PERSPECTIVES ON DEVELOPMENT

Perspectives on Development

Memoirs of a Development Economist

V.V. Bhatt

ACADEMIC FOUNDATION
NEW DELHI

Cover: Chinese painting by Prafulla Bhatt

First published in 2008
by

ACADEMIC FOUNDATION
4772-73 / 23 Bharat Ram Road, (23 Ansari Road),
Darya Ganj, New Delhi - 110 002 (India).
Phones : 23245001 / 02 / 03 / 04.
Fax : +91-11-23245005.
E-mail : academic@vsnl.com
www. academicfoundation.com

Cataloging in Publication Data--DK
Courtesy: D.K. Agencies (P) Ltd. <docinfo@dkagencies.com>

Bhatt, V. V. (Vinayak Vijayshanker)
Perspectives on development : memoirs of a development economist / V.V. Bhatt
p. cm.
ISBN 13: 9788171886838
ISBN 10: 8171886833

1. Bhatt, V. V. (Vinayak Vijayshanker). 2. Economists --India--Biography. 3. Development economics--India. 4. India--Economic conditions--20th century. 5. India—Economic policy--1947- I. Title.

DDC 338.954 22

Typeset by Italics India, New Delhi.
Printed and bound in India.

For Swati, Gita and Shuchi

शिवाः ते पन्थानः सन्तु

Contents

Acknowledgements

I would not have attempted to write these memoirs if my friends—Anand Chandravarkar and Deena Khatkhate had not insisted repeatedly on my doing so. Both read my first draft and made several suggestions. Mr. Arthur Monteiro of Delhi not only typed my manuscript but also suggested several editorial changes. My daughter Gita, who works at the IMF, helped me in several ways—receiving and sending e-mails, making corrections and suggesting some editorial changes. Mr. Rituraj Kapila responded very graciously to my request for publication of my these memoirs.

I am very grateful to all of them

V.V. Bhatt

Preface

I have called these memoirs *Perspectives on Development* for several reasons. India was the first developing country to think about development for eliminating poverty, attain full employment and improving living standards. In fact, the struggle for political independence had its rationale for this purpose. There was rigorous discussion with regard to development strategy and policies and for this purpose, the Congress party appointed a National Planning Committee, under the chairmanship of Jawaharlal Nehru. In the discussions at the committee, a consensus had emerged with regard to the choice of a development strategy and later on it became the cornerstone of development planning after Independence. Thus, a number of young students got interested in economics and had a missionary zeal to participate in the development process. It was in this milieu that I grew up and developed an interest in economics in order to participate in some way in this venture (Chapter 1).

So I studied Economics both at Bombay and Harvard; my major purpose was to equip myself as a development economist. At Harvard, I had very eminent teachers like Schumpeter, Leontief and Gerschenkron and they had profound insights into the development process, based on their study of the economic history of Europe and even other countries. With all that I learned from them, I chose as the theme of my dissertation for Ph.D. degree, employment and capital formation in underdeveloped economies. This thesis in fact anticipated the development strategy adopted by India for its Second Five-year Plan (Chapter 2).

With this training, I joined the Reserve Bank of India; its Research Department was a premier and prestigious centre for research on economic problems and policies in India. I worked on several themes related to development planning. Initially I analysed the planning process with regard to the second five-year plan. I pointed out that its specific output targets were not based on sound planning techniques based on input-output analysis, it ignored the resources constraint—both with regard to domestic and foreign exchange resources—and its reliance on deficit financing that would result in inflation. I anticipated that all these were bound to result in a control regime, inimical to the emergence of private entrepreneurs, as it did.

Then I concentrated on improving the database for planning. First I attempted to make the estimates of saving and investment, then a study of the pattern of income distribution and develop a technique for financial planning. All these studies were published in the *Reserve Bank Bulletin* as pioneering studies on these themes.

At the instance of the Governor of the Reserve Bank, I commented on the draft Fourth Plan, pointed out that its output targets for several sectors and more particularly on power were based on inadequate data, that it did not consider the resources constraint and could not be viable on the basis of domestic and foreign exchange resources. The Governor liked my comments and sent them to the Planning Commission. This created a stir in the Commission and they had to revise their output targets as well as the availability of resources.

Later on, I was a member of the Resources Working Group, chaired by I.G. Patel, and in this capacity I developed a technique of flow-of-funds for financial planning. This report was discussed at the meeting of the group and was accepted as a viable basis for financial planning (Chapter 3).

As Chief Executive of the Industrial Development Bank of India, I gave a significant development orientation to its policies. I evolved a number of measures to strengthen its promotional function to initiate a viable and self-reinforcing process of industrial development (Chapter 4).

At the Asian Institute of Economic Development and Planning, I concentrated on development issues for the seminars I conducted for senior officials of the governments of Asian countries. I developed a curriculum for a course on development for this purpose. In this connection, I held several seminars not only at Bangkok but also in Taiwan, Indonesia and Iran. I also worked on "A Framework for Planned Economic Development for Lower Mekong Countries." This monograph was discussed at the Institute as well as at ECAFE and both arranged a seminar on this monograph. Both ECAFE and the Institute not only approved of the study but persuaded the countries concerned to work on the project (Chapter 5).

At the World Bank, I was involved in research on themes like financial structure and policies and public enterprise management. These were also the themes I introduced for seminars for senior officials of governments, along with a seminar for chief executives of development banks. Thus for the Economic Development Institute (EDI), I introduced three novel themes: development banking, financial innovations, technology policy and project evaluation and public enterprise management. For the seminars, I wrote several research papers; they were used for the EDI seminars (Chapter 6).

As an independent consultant, I reviewed the functioning of financial system in Sri Lanka to suggest necessary institutional changes; this was at the request of the Sri Lanka government. Later on I worked as a consultant to the EDI and participated in the projects on the Main Bank System in Japan and its relevance for developing countries, Japanese civil service and development, and linkage of rural industrial development with urban commerce and industry.

Then I worked on the theme of improving the effectiveness and efficiency of the financial system in India as a consultant to the Indian Council for Research on International Relations (ICRIER); this monograph was published by the ICRIER.

At the request of I.G. Patel to deliver a paper on perspectives on development for the annual session of the Gujarat Economic Association, I worked on the theme on which I had thought for a long time since my Harvard days (Chapter 7).

I was associated with Indian planning and wondered why India did not experience a much more rapid growth than it did, in spite of its rich development potential. I dealt with this theme even in my earlier papers. My view was that socialist ideology instead of being an instrument of development after 1964-65 resulted in a licence-control regime, inimical to the emergence of private entrepreneurs. The mindset of politicians and civil servants became anti-business and this resulted in multiplication of control and regulations till 1985–1990. Since then, several reforms were initiated in 1990 and the old regime of licence-permit *raj* was discarded and a positive attitude towards private entrepreneurs emerged. The reform process still continues and promises to initiate a vigorous self-reinforcing process of industrial and economic development (Chapter 8).

The final chapter presents a theme in which I was interested since my training as a development economist, related to profound insights into the development process in economic literature since Adam Smith.

Thus, I was engaged throughout my career on problems of development and policies; hence the title of these memoirs as *Perspectives on Development*. This subjective account based on personal experience may help economic historians as it may shed light on certain events that cannot be captured by objective data.

1

Salt Satyagraha and After (1930–1946)

THE twenties of the last century were an eventful decade from the point of view of India's Independence movement. The Indian leaders had expected that Britain would grant dominion status to India after the moral and material help it gave the British during the First World War. This hope was dashed by the British response to the Rowlatt Acts and the Jalianwala Bagh episode. All leaders were disillusioned with British justice and fair play. Gandhiji in particular, who had a great regard for British justice, was aghast at this turn of events. Hence he assumed the leadership of the Congress party, remodelled it as a mass party, and announced that India had no option but to start a non-cooperation movement to gain freedom. A mass movement was to be launched to gain *swaraj* in one year. The whole nation was aroused and the leadership was prepared for this movement.

However, the Chauri-Choura episode—in which a police station and its inmates were burnt—convinced Gandhiji that the movement would not remain non-violent and hence he abruptly suspended the non-cooperation fight. He said that his was a Himalayan blunder in expecting that India was prepared for non-violent non-cooperation. The Congress leaders, and in particular Jawaharlal Nehru, were appalled at Gandhiji's move simply because in one village some violence occurred.

Very soon Gandhiji was arrested and charged with sedition. This was the first and last court case in which he was tried. He pleaded guilty and charged the British with having completely emasculating the nation with their repressive policies that he had no other option but to resort to seditious activities. He told the judge, Bromfield, that if he were convinced of his reasoning, he should resign from his post or give him a maximum sentence under British law. The judge was highly respectful about the integrity and character of the saintly leader; however under the law, he had to sentence him to six years imprisonment. This sentence was similar to the one meted out to another great leader, Bal Gangadhar Tilak, some years earlier. This case was reminiscent of the famous trial of Socrates. Gandhiji had translated Plato's description of this trial in Gujarati while he was leading the movement for the rights of Indians in South Africa. The nation was so much aroused by this trial that the British never again tried Gandhiji in court. In later years he was imprisoned several times but without a court trial.

With Gandhiji's imprisonment there was a lull in the freedom movement. Some Congress leaders, including Motilal Nehru, were eager to fight elections to the central and provincial legislatures and strive for freedom by working within the government. Proponents of this idea were called "Swarajists."

Gandhiji did not believe that council entry would be effective in attaining independence. His view was that if Indians remained fearless, strong and united and practiced non-violence, which is a quality of the brave, independence would be attained sooner than by any other means. His emphasis was on examining religious, social and cultural practices and beliefs in the light of reason and intelligence. All those practices like untouchability and caste divisions, which did not pass the test of reason, had to be abolished. He also advocated that India should strive for economic reform by encouraging village industries such as hand spinning and weaving which could provide employment to the idle hands during the non-agricultural seasons. One should not have to rely on the government for such radical reforms. He did not want independence for its own sake but to abolish poverty and irrational beliefs and practices; and also for equipping India to strive for world peace and prosperity. He was open to all ideas and practices from outside India that would promote India's freedom as well as world peace. He believed in *Vasudaiva Kutumbakam*—all earth belongs to humanity as a family. For him, non-violence was the way to search for truth. Truth for him was God.

However, the younger generation of the Congress, led by Jawaharlal Nehru, believed in attaining complete freedom and were opposed to council entry. Gandhiji was neutral in the matter and let the Swarajists have their way.

Jawaharlal did not want dominion status; he was for complete independence—*Poorna Swaraj*. This he advocated when he became the Congress president, succeeding his father Motilal Nehru. Gandhiji advocated caution and suggested waiting for one year. If within a year Britain did not grant dominion status, the Congress should then declare its aim as complete independence. Nehru was persuaded. At the end of one year when there was no change in India's status, the Congress declared its aim as complete independence. 26 January, 1930 was declared as Independence Day and was celebrated with vigour and enthusiasm throughout India. (This date is now celebrated as Republic Day, which coincided with the day on which India adopted its present constitution after Independence, on 26 January, 1951.)

Gandhiji was appointed as the leader to start the non-violent movement for independence. He was at that time in his *Ashram* at Ahmedabad, where he settled after returning from South Africa. He waited for his inner voice to suggest the course of action.

It was at this time that I saw Gandhiji at his prayer meeting. I was taken there by my father. I was about three and a half years old. I vividly remember his serene and pensive face. This was some time after 26 January 1930, when he was searching for a way to lead the independence movement. Soon, his inner voice suggested that he should break the law on salt manufacture. This was a state monopoly and he wanted people to break this monopoly by manufacturing salt, a principal item of diet for the poor as well as the cattle. Thus was to start what is known as the "Salt Satyagraha." Before starting this movement, as was his practice, he wrote a letter to his friend—Viceroy Irwin—inviting him to take certain measures towards granting dominion status to India. If these demands were not met, he said, he would be constrained to start the independence movement by breaking the law on salt. This was on 2 March 1930. When these demands were not met, he decided to break the salt law and urged all Congress members and others to do likewise. On 12 March he started on foot from Ahmedabad to Dundee, where he would disobey this law on 5 April. The British were amused at such manner of starting a movement, with what they considered a ridiculous and amusing gesture.

However, this ignited such a powerful spark that all Indians—including women and children—were inspired with great vigour, enthusiasm and courage to join the movement by boycotting British textiles and goods, taking to spinning and wearing *khadi* and giving up ornaments. There were nationwide processions. The foreign press reporters, particularly from the United States, were astonished at this unique non-violent struggle. Soon Gandhiji was imprisoned and Sarojini Naidu assumed leadership of the Congress party and marched with several *satyagrahis* to Dharasana to break the salt law. The foreign reporters were surprised at the way they fearlessly faced brutal *lathi* charges by soldiers on foot and horse. Several heads were broken, several were injured. Still there was no violence. There was only the determination to face violent and brutal attacks. Meanwhile, all prominent Congress leaders—Motilal Nehru, Jawaharlal Nehru, Vallabhbhai Patel, Rajendra Prasad and several others were arrested. The world was stunned at this fearless non-violent movement and the brutality with which the British responded.

Several of my family members, including my mother and my father's sisters, took to spinning and *khadi*. My uncle—my father's sister's husband—took an active part in the protests and was arrested and sent to jail in Nashik. My cousin was arrested in our village—Umreth, near Dakor—and all women and children went to the railway station to garland him and sang in a circle the song "May our flag soar high in the sky" and shouted the slogan "Inqlab Zindabad" ("Let revolution spread"). I was part of this group and was infected with the exuberance of the participants.

My grandfather took his family—his daughters, son-in-law, my father and mother and his grandchildren—to Nashik jail to visit his son-in-law. A few days later, we received the sad news of my grandmother's demise at Umreth. We bathed in the Godavari river and prayed for the repose of her soul. My father, her only son, felt totally orphaned at her passing away. Later on, whenever he recited to us a poem by Kalapi on a mother's death, his face would be tearful. Later on, he would recite to us several devotional songs from Gandhiji's *Ashram Bhajanawali*. He also made us familiar with the Bhagavad Gita and taught us to recite the sixteenth *adhyay* of this Celestial Song. Later on, when one of my teachers at school recited the first *adhyay* where Arjun is sad and not prepared to fight his relatives and elders, Arjun's dilemma became heartrending. Such was our introduction to the *Gita*. Its verses reverberate in my mind and the *Gita* has been with us all our life. Much later, after reading a poetic commentary on the *Gita* by Kishorelal Mashruwala, a Gandhian and an independent thinker, I wrote on the message of this Celestial Song. Mashruwala later on also edited the *Harijan*, a weekly founded by Gandhiji, after Gandhiji's death. I could recite several *adhyays* of this beautiful and moving song, which is the essence of the *Upanishads*, which are a source of all Indian religious-philosophical thought—of all the religions that originated in India, Buddhism, Jainism, Sikhism and the several branches of what is now known as Hinduism. Edwin Arnold translated it into English as *Song Celestial*, a song for all humanity.

My grandfather—we called him Papaji—was born in 1864. He respected Gandhiji but did not approve of his mass movements. These spread lawlessness, he said. Coming from a poor family, he had experienced the blessings of the British *raj* and had become a part of the judiciary. His parents had no land or assets. But his mother was ambitious and induced him to study. He walked several miles to school. With persistence, he graduated from Elphinstone College in Bombay, benefiting from the philanthropy of Gokaldas Tejpal. Gokaldas had started a boarding house for deserving students at Grant Road, about five miles away from Elphinstone College. My grandfather walked this distance to and from college. Later on, several eminent persons, including Morarji Desai, also took advantage of this facility.

After graduation, grandfather took up a job as translator at the Bombay High Court. In his spare time he studied Law. After his law degree, he was appointed a judge. In this capacity he worked at various places in Maharashtra and Gujarat. He had a tremendous reputation as an impartial judge. In Kaira district he was called Manchharam Munsaf. His village honoured him as the first graduate and judge from the village. He was promoted later as an Assistant District Judge. Because of his reputation, a British District Judge recommended him, after his retirement, as liquidator of a textile mill of the Lalbhai Group.

With this background, he believed in British justice and fair play and disapproved of mass movements of the kind started by Gandhiji. However, he did not prevent his son, his son-in-law and grandchildren from participating in Gandhiji's various activities.

He was an independent thinker. At one time in his life he became an atheist. He was against superstitious practices whether of the religious or socio-cultural nature. He advocated social reform—against child marriage, in favour of widow remarriage, against lavish caste dinners and the practice of dowry, which impoverishes the parents of daughters. He became the first president of an organisation for social reform. His inspiration for these activities came from Mahadev Govind Ranade, K.T. Telang, Gopalkrishna Gokhale, Dalapatram Kavi—father of the great poet of Gujarat, Nanalal—and Narsimharao Divatia, a government official as also a great poet. He favoured education for girls and induced all those who came in contact with him to study hard and take advantage of educational opportunities.

He advised us (me, my brothers and sister) to study hard and later on to write on interesting themes and engage in research for this purpose. He was not for amassing money but urged us to devote ourselves to intellectual pursuits. He favoured a frugal and economical life; he would chide us if we left the water tap running idly.

In his retirement years, while we were in high school, he made us (because of his weak eyesight) read aloud to him the *Times of India*, which improved our English, as also Gujarati literature. My father read to him several historical books, including the literature on the 1857 Indian war of independence; my father was well read about the events of 1857, and on the centenary of this event wrote a book on the subject in Gujarati. This reading aloud was part of our education.

While my elder brother and I were in high school, my father took great interest in our education and arranged for a separate room in our small house for our study. Later on, he used his assets to send my brother and me to study at Harvard. His friends advised him to use his money to make more money and not to be extravagant about his children's education. How much money are your sons going to make after their education? They argued. My father, however, wanted to equip us for an educational career and to take part in India's socio-economic development after Independence. It was because of his encouragement and parsimonious living that my elder brother could take an MBA from Harvard, I a Ph.D from Harvard and my youngest brother could study medicine.

Like his father, my father was an active social reformer. For cultivating public opinion, he wrote articles for socio-cultural reform in various Gujarati journals—*Shikshan Ane Sahitya, Jyohirdhar* and our caste magazine—and also gave lectures. After high school, I also took to writing on several reform themes. All our extended family members were also associated with the social reform movement. My father was truly religious but did not believe in going to temples or other religious rituals. He knew that all temple activities were based on superstition and even corruption. My grandfather was an atheist at one time but later on was attracted by Sahajanand Swami, a great religious-social reformer and mystic from north India settled in Gujarat-Saurashtra, and was also an adviser to the *acharya* of the Ahmedabad temple. My father was not impressed by the *acharya* and never came with us to this temple even on our New Year day. My grandfather knew by heart the *Vishnu Sahastra Nam* and recited it every day. Knowing that his son would not do so, he urged my mother to recite this everyday, which she did till the end of her life in 1989.

On the world scene, the Second World War was about to start. Most Indian leaders were eager to participate in this war if the British promised independence after the war. Gandhiji was not in favour of disrupting the war effort and in a sense left the Congress. The Congress leadership tried to convince the British of their cause and were willing to support the war if they were associated with the war effort. Roosevelt had declared the Four Freedoms for all countries after the war, but Winston Churchill did not want to give this pledge to Indians, in spite of Roosevelt's advocacy. Thus, there was a stalemate and the Congress leadership had to invite Gandhiji to lead them.

Gandhiji was in favour of giving moral support to the Allies and non-violent resistance to the Axis powers. He did not favour a mass movement that might adversely affect the war effort of the Allies. So he thought of individual civil disobedience, a symbolic gesture for gaining independence. He chose Vinoba Bhave as the first *satyagrahi* and Jawaharlal Nehru as the second. Both were arrested as also others who followed. Again there was a stalemate and the British government sent Stafford Cripps to negotiate a settlement but without the authority to accept the Congress demand for independence after the end of the war.

Meanwhile the Allies suffered setbacks in the war and Japan took Burma and was at the doorstep of India. The Japanese were supported by Subhas Chandra Bose, who had escaped prison and had raised the Indian National Army that was meant to fight alongside the Japanese to invade India. The situation was grave, with the possibility of Indians siding with the Japanese and accepting Japanese rule. This would have been tantamount to changing masters. This, Gandhiji thought, would be disastrous for the Indian independence movement. Such an outcome had to be resisted by arousing Indians to fight for immediate independence so that they could fight even the Japanese if they invaded India. So he gave a call for Quit India movement, asking the British to leave India and let the Indians fight for freedom from whatever source their freedom was threatened. On 8 August 1942, the Congress passed the resolution and appointed Gandhiji to negotiate with the British before starting any mass movement. But before he had a chance to do so, he along with the entire Congress leadership were arrested and the British resolved to suppress any movement ruthlessly—which Gandhiji described in his letter to the Viceroy as LIONINE And This Is What They Did. Now without any leadership, people took to measures that they thought fit.

Jayaprakash Narayan, Achyut Patwardhan and others led people to destroy railways, telegraph communications and the like without resorting to violence against individuals and government officials. Gandhiji in his letter to the Viceroy condemned those actions as being violent. But he said these actions were the result of British violence against the people.

Along with others, we participated in the Quit India movement. We left our studies, joined processions and tried to cultivate public opinion for non-violent resistance to the British. My father started a hand-written newsletter. We took 10-11 copies of this letter and distributed it to others, who in turn took copies, and so on. So it went on for over a year. Meanwhile my grandfather passed away and I felt I should actively join in the movement. On the ninth of every month—as the movement started on 9 August—there was a procession led by some individuals challenging the police to arrest them. In April 1943, I joined three others in leading such a procession to face the armed police. We were all arrested. The police were willing to release me if I apologised for my behaviour. This was at the instance of my cousin, who was a judge and a prominent lawyer friend of the family. I refused and was brought before the court. In view of my age—I was fourteen—the judge sentenced me to two months' imprisonment and sent me to Sabarmati jail in Ahmedabad.

The jail was overcrowded with political prisoners of all ages. Jail authorities were lenient as they could not maintain law and order without the cooperation of the prisoners (and they knew that independence was not far off). This was unlike the thirties, when prisoners were subjected to hard labour. We had study circles. One was for the reading of Gandhiji's thought, organised by the veteran, much-respected Ravishankar Maharaj, a fearless Gandhian who converted several tribes of dacoits and robbers. A second study circle was by Babalbai Mehta, a veteran Gandhian who organised villagers in Thamana (near my village) for socioeconomic reform. He read to us the biography by the Eastern and Western disciples of Vivekananda. A third study circle was by Ravajibhai Patel, who spoke to us about the *satyagraha* in South Africa, in which he had participated. In all these study circles, while listening to the readings and lectures we spun on our spinning wheels. G.V. Mavalankar—who later became the first Speaker of the Lok Sabha—was in B class prison. Since he knew my family, he invited me to meet him on occasions. Ravishanker Maharaj knew me as a grandson of Manchharam Mansaf. Such was our education in human values, which should govern any good society.

We had a sort of corn soup in the morning, and lunch and supper of a millet loaf. Once a week, we were given onions and *gur* with the millet loaf. On payment, which my father arranged, I was given a glass of milk. Once it was poisoned (by accident). When I woke up in the morning, I found several prisoners in the hospital; because of my sound sleep, I was somehow not affected. I formed friendships with several prisoners. One of them was Jayant Thakker, who was a medical student but later on because of poverty could not pursue his studies and started a business in surgical instruments. He has since been a family friend. My father-in-law, when he was transferred to Madras in the early sixties, stayed with him and both became close friends. Now he has retired and is staying at Aurobindo Ashram in Pondicherry, leaving his business to his brothers.

So the days passed. I was released from jail before the academic year began and I rejoined the S.L.D. Arts College at Ahmedabad in my second year of the college.

In my first year at this college, before 1942, I had the good fortune of having very good teachers. In particular, I remember my Gujarati teacher, Ramarayan Pathak—a very well known critic, poet, and short story writer—who introduced us to Gujarati as well as Sanskrit literature. He is respected as the doyen of Gujarati literature of the Gandhiyuga in Gujarat. My Sanskrit teacher taught me Kalidasa's *Meghdut*. He would first recite a stanza, then recite the Gujarati version—of Kilabhai Ghanshyam Bhatt—and then comment on it. By this time, I would have already memorised it. In fact, I knew several stanzas by heart, which my teacher appreciated. In Civics, V.K.R.V. Rao gave profound lectures. In Mathematics, I had a Cambridge wrangler as a teacher of Calculus and Sandhil for Algebra and one for Solid Geometry, who while entering the class would be singing verses from Jaydev.

Thus after release from jail, my studies began in earnest, with specialisation in Economics, which has remained my subject since then. For, I wanted to devote my time to thinking about the socio-economic development of India. One influence at that time was a lecture by K.T. Shah on the work of the National Planning Committee, appointed by Subhas Chandra Bose when he was president of the Congress, and was chaired by Jawaharlal Nehru. The deliberations of this committee, with members from different strata of socioeconomic classes of India, had more or less agreed on the strategy for economic development, without any ideological bias. Of course, with Jawaharlal Nehru and K.T. Shah there was an emphasis on the necessity of policies towards an Indian version of socialism. On Gandhiji's emphasis on poverty elimination, village development and employment there was no dispute. However, what the committee wanted was rapid industrialisation, based on science and technology, and for this purpose an active role of the state in developing basic industries. We as students agreed more with Jawaharlal Nehru than with Gandhiji's emphasis *only* on village development and cottage industries. At this time socialism as an ideology merely meant the importance of the state in initiating and supporting modern industries, in particular the basic industries and economic infrastructure. Even well-established industrialists supported this strategy.

2

Learning Economics: Bombay and Harvard (1946–1952)

WHEN I rejoined college, V.K.R.V. Rao was the first principal at a very young age of about 25 years. He wore *khadi* and argued that *khadi* was competitive with mill cloth. He did not believe that students should give up socio-cultural activities simply because national political leaders were in jail. He said that we should not be solemn and refuse to enjoy life. He had great faith in Ramakrishna Paramahamsa and Vivekananda; he gave several public lectures on these two and their thoughts, which were consistent with the Indian heritage of *Upanishads* and the *Gita*. He was an eloquent speaker. Once when S. Radhakrishnan came to our college he introduced him with great eloquence for about fifty-five minutes, while Radhakrishnan spoke in his measured tones for only thirty minutes.

Dr. Rao was one of the first Indians to study Economics at Cambridge, where he was awarded a Ph.D. degree for his research on Indian national income; this was pioneering research when there was no work done on national income after Dadabhai Naoroji in the late nineteenth century. For this he was awarded the much-coveted Adam Smith Prize. He was a student of Keynes and Keynes was impressed by his studies as well as his contribution in discussions on various themes in Keynes' seminars (only the best students were permitted to attend these seminars). Keynes was of the opinion that he would be the finance minister after India's independence.

After returning to India, Rao was invited to become the first principal of the S.L.D. Arts College. This college was established by the Kasturbhai Group at the instance of B.K. Mazumdar (who worked with Kasturbhai, a well-known and public-spirited industrialist) who had studied at the London School and was keen to establish colleges of excellence in Ahmedabad. At that time because of the independence movement, good students did not go to government colleges like the Gujarat College, and most of them joined the S.L.D. Arts College with its brilliant staff and a charismatic principal. I joined this college when V.K.R.V. Rao was the principal. Later on Rao started several institutions to train economists to do research on Indian economic problems and policies to help the process of economic development and planning. These institutions were: Delhi School of Economics, Institute of Economic Growth and a Bangalore institute. He attracted bright economists to work in these institutions like Amartya Sen, Jagdish Bhagwati, Sukhamoy Chakravarti and a very senior economist, K.N. Raj. Thus, he performed with enormous energy and effort the function of contributing to India's development, which was his passion.

B.R. Shenoy became the next principal. He was a very good teacher. With great clarity he introduced us to Hayek's *Prices and Production* and Keynes' second volume of *Treatise on Money*, which dealt with credit creation by the banking system, currency standards and his proposal for an international monetary institution, a forerunner of the International Monetary Fund. He was a student of Hayek at the London School and was greatly influenced by Hayek's contributions to economics and public policy; however, he did not appreciate Keynes' General Theory, which he did not mention to us.

This was a time when some well-known Indian industrialists like Tata, Birla, Goenka, Kasturbhai Lalbhai and some others formulated a strategy of economic development with their Bombay Plan. Shenoy was critical of their approach as leading to deficit financing and inflation and explained his reasoning to us. He also introduced us to the discussions at Bretton Woods and the plans by Keynes and White. He wrote two books, one on *Postwar Depression and Way out* and *Sterling Assets of India*. He lectured to us on these themes in simple language but with great clarity. He also introduced us to Hayek's *Road to Serfdom*. He believed in free enterprise and was averse to government controls and intervention, which stifled entrepreneurial initiative and thus economic development.

Apart from him, we did not have good teachers in Theory of Value or Micro-economics. We relied on our own reading—books by Benham and Meade. I read Keynes' *General Theory* and in particular his liquidity preference theory for the rate of interest. Shenoy did not refer to this book but I found it very illuminating and absorbing. *General Theory* appealed to me because of its common sense and its rejection of orthodox economic doctrine, which believed in the self-correcting mechanism of markets, in spite of the fact of the Great Depression and unemployment in all the industrialised countries.

On India's economic problems I read Jathar and Beri and Wadia and Merchant. The former presented India's economic problems in a balanced and exhaustive manner; the latter had an ideological bent. We understood these problems from our own observation and study of Indian economic history. These problems persisted after independence and many of them are still with us—all relating to rural development and unemployment. Anyway, I did not rely on teachers; I did my own reading and understood what Gandhiji stood for—industrialisation of the village.

In 1943, Mahatma Gandhi's elocution competition was started for the colleges of Gujarat. In the first competition in 1943, I.G. Patel won the gold medal and a trophy along with Nalini Ambegaokar.

I.G. later on went to Cambridge for his Ph.D. degree. He was awarded the much-coveted Adam Smith Prize for his brilliance. He was a student of Keynes. Later on he was invited by Professor Anjaria to join as Deputy Economic Adviser in the Ministry of Finance. He became Economic Secretary in the Ministry in spite of the strong opposition from the IAS lobby; he was the first economist to become a Secretary in the government, even though he was not IAS. Because of his intellectual status and charming personality, the Indian economists regarded him as the doyen of economists—a Guru in Sanskrit language.

Nalini Ambegaokar later on became my colleague at the Reserve Bank of India as head of the Division of Banking.

In 1945, I was selected to represent our college along with H.N. Pathak. Pathak got the gold medal and we two won the trophy. Shenoy was indeed very glad and came to the stage to congratulate me. In the next year, I won the gold medal. Professor Junankar, who had a Ph.D. in Philosophy from Oxford, trained us for such competitions.

In 1946, I obtained the Bachelor of Arts degree in Economics, obtaining a first class, much to my surprise. Dharma Kumar stood first and Nadkarni third, myself being the second. Dharma later became my colleague at the Reserve Bank of India and Lovraj Kumar and she became my friends. Later on she went to Cambridge for her Ph.D. and on her return joined the Delhi School of Economics as Professor of Economic History. There she started an excellent journal, *Indian Economic and Social History Review*. Nadkarni joined the Bombay School of Economics, when he asked for my advice whether he should pursue his studies at the school or join the Imperial Bank of India, where he had been selected as an officer. I told him that since he had no academic ambition, he should join the much-coveted job, which he did. Later on he became Chairman of the bank in its new *avatar* as the nationalised State Bank of India.

My father and my cousin (almost as old as my father) wanted me to pursue postgraduate studies at the Bombay School. I followed their advice without any great ambition, except to do well in studies. It was difficult to stay in Bombay unless I could get admission to the University Hostel, which had 10 seats for Economics and 10 for Chemical Technology. I applied for admission but the hostel rector, Professor C.N. Vakil, would not let a student know the status of application by letter. One of my relations went to the notice board, found out that I was admitted, and informed me at Ahmedabad.

I sent a cheque to Professor Vakil for the hostel fees. When I went to the hostel, he called me and said with feigned anger why I had sent a cheque and other papers by post. "Why didn't you realise that I have no secretarial assistance to receive such post?" he asked. I merely said that I was not informed about my admission and how to pay the fees. Later on, he would tell us hostel students how to behave, to take permission if we were to go out of Bombay, to be back at the hostel before 9.30 p.m., etc. Once I was late by 10 minutes and went to him to explain. He just nodded and later on told the prefect, H.N. Pathak, to inform me that I should not bother him if I was late by a few minutes.

I had a room with two partners. R.M. Honavar was a Ph.D. student. He later on became the Chief Economic Adviser in the

Ministry of Finance. K.M. Bhourasker, the other roommate, was also a Ph.D. student. He later on retired as Collector in Indore. Since both of them left the room early in the morning, the entire room was mine to study undisturbed. Honavar was reserved and K.M. was sociable when he was free.

H.N. Pathak was senior to me at S.L.D. Arts College. We had together won the Gandhi trophy. He was a very good student. Later on he joined the Indian Institute of Management, Ahmedabad, after doing his Master's from the London School of Economics. The other Ph.D. students were B.V. Krishnamurthy, K.S. Krishnaswami and P.R. Brahmananda. B.V. wrote his thesis on "Pricing in a Planned Economy" (which was a clear exposition of the problem). He also taught us Hicks' *Value and Capital* with great clarity of presentation. Brahmananda was a great scholar, particularly well versed in the classics (Adam Smith, Ricardo, etc.). Later on he wrote several books. One of them, co-authored with Prof. C.N. Vakil on *Planning for an Expanding Economy,* was an illuminating critique of the Second Plan and became well-known as an alternative strategy for development. He retired as Director of the Bombay School. K.S. Krishnaswami was doing his Ph.D. at the school and also taught us monetary theory. He left the Bombay School to study at the London School for his Ph.D. and later on joined the Reserve Bank, then the Planning Commission, and retired as Deputy Governor of the Reserve Bank.

This was the time when the Bombay School was one of the two institutions devoted to postgraduate studies in economics. The other was the Gokhale Institute in Poona with a very eminent economist (Professor Gadgil) as director. Gadgil himself had done considerable work on Indian economic history as well as on economic problems, particularly in rural areas, and policies of India. He was succeeded by V.M. Dandekar, an economist of rare critical intelligence and understanding of India's economic problems.

Gadgil initiated the work in the Reserve Bank on Rural Credit Survey and was the principal author of this committee's report. This was the first time when rural problems were tackled in a significant manner. This was due to the initiatives of Gadgil and supported actively by the Reserve Bank, whose contribution has not been recognised even in the *History of the Reserve Bank* (there are three volumes now of the *History*). Morarji Desai, when he was Finance

Minister, requested Gadgil to become Deputy Chairman of the Planning Commission, where he worked on India's economic policies. Somehow, when Indira Gandhi became the Prime Minister, she did not like any experts with independent thought, who might not agree with her policies and politics. Disillusioned, Gadgil left Delhi and on the way in the train near Surat (where he had worked in a college in his early days), he collapsed partly as a result of his treatment in Delhi.

The Gokhale Institute devoted itself to empirical work on India's problems. However, the Bombay School was the only institution which concentrated its attention on postgraduate studies and research. Hence all the students of economics from all parts of India, who desired to do postgraduate work joined the Bombay School. For example, B.V., K.S. and Brahmananda came from Bangalore after their studies at the Mysore University. Earlier, V.K.R.V. Rao and I.G. Patel had joined the School for their research; later on, however, they left for Cambridge for further studies. Such was the reputation of the School. I joined the School after my B.A. degree.

Initially, the School had good professors like Anjaria, Dantwala, Lakdawala and some others. But except Dantwala who guided students in agricultural economics and policy, the rest did not bring enough expertise or experience to guide research students. Those who did Ph.D. at the School worked on their own without much guidance. Even teaching at the School was not inspiring except for that of Anjaria, Dantwala and Lakdawala.

Professor Vakil, who was Director of the School, had a feudal temperament and did not encourage bright economists, who might disagree with him on some issues, to join the School. He did not even attract bright young economists, who returned after their studies abroad, as V.K.R.V. Rao did, for the Delhi School.

So the Bombay School with all its early reputation lost its importance as a centre for postgraduate studies, particularly after C.N. Vakil left.

Vakil had a Ph.D. from the London School, under the guidance of Vera Enstey, who liked Indian students. On his return, he became the Director of the School. He had a number of good students, who did Ph.D. but he published several studies done by his students with claim to be the first co-author. Thus, there were books by Vakil and

Murngan, Vakil and Anjaria, Vakil and Brahmananda, and so on. This reminded one of Professor Harris at Harvard, where I later on studied. All this is typical of Indian tradition, which is somehow not capable of maintaining and improving institutions after the founding leaders leave the scene, unlike Oxford, Cambridge, Harvard and the rest in Europe and the United States.

The hostel was in a dilapidated building near Marine Lines station. The rooms were poorly lit and one got a smell of fish from the building at the back. The dining room was dingy. Because of rationing, we got millet loaf, rice and *dal*. There was a tea-caterer, Bhat. He was very active in serving tea at whatever time one wanted, with a smile and a song (from the famous Gujarati poet Zaverchand Meghani). Since he was near the only phone booth we had, he would rush to tell us about any phone calls coming to us (which were eagerly awaited). None of us complained about our amenities; for to have a place in Bombay to study was itself a blessing.

One incident, however, was quite exasperating. At the time of our final examination, there was no water and we had to make do with a pail of water. At the same time it was found that our cook had syphilis; so there was no food as well. But being completely absorbed in our studies for the examination, we stoically took this in our stride.

In my second year at the hostel, we were joined by Bharat Desai (a cousin of Prof. C.N. Vakil). After his Ph.D. he became principal of a government college. The other was Deena Khatkhate, a serious student who used to discuss economics and economic policies with me on our regular walks up to Nariman Point. On our way back, we would have a cup of coffee at what was at that time Parisian Restaurant. Once we had no money to pay for the coffee and had to deposit our watches as collateral before we paid the dues. Later on, he was my colleague at the Reserve Bank of India. His thesis on monetary policy in developing countries became a textbook for students at the school, as is mentioned by one student. Later on, he joined the International Monetary Fund. We have been good friends since our student days and in Washington, we continue to remember our early years (of fun and gossip) along with our friend A.G. Chandavarkar (a student at the school before I joined it and later on our colleague at the Reserve Bank) who also worked at the IMF. He had a B.Sc. degree with high honours from the London School. Later on he wrote on several themes on monetary theory and central banking. He is still very active in writing. Recently, after his famous book on *Keynes and India,* he has written on the reform of the Reserve Bank of India, advocating its independence from politics and government intervention.

At the Bombay School, the one teacher whom I remember very well was J.J. Anjaria. In my first term, he gave very lucid lectures in Keynes' *Treatise* and *General Theory*. In our School journal he wrote an article on the relevance of Keynes to India and argued convincingly that India's problem of employment was not the same as analysed by Keynes. Much before A.K. Dasgupta and V.K.R.V. Rao, he had dealt with this problem with great clarity and lucidity. Once I wrote a paper on Howtrey (whom I had studied very well). To my annoyance he thought that I could not have written such an excellent paper and must have plagiarised some other author. This was unlike him and I was aghast at such a remark. Anyway, he left the School and joined the Reserve Bank of India and from there was deputed to the Ministry of Finance and Planning Commission as Chief Economic Adviser. The First Five Year Plan which he drafted gave a lucid and incisive account of the discussion on planning and development that preceded independence as well as the approaches of Gandhiji and Nehru and the National Planning Committee and other plans. No other Plan document since, has equalled it for clarity, lucidity and depth. I.G. Patel described it as being similar to the epic *Mahabharat*: whatever problems India faced were elegantly presented there and whatever was not in it was not relevant for India either. For understanding the vigorous discussion and debates that took place in India before independence about socio-economic development, no other document can match it. Economists refer to the Harrod-Domar model as a planning device, as mentioned in the Plan by economists who had recently learnt about it. But this was merely an ornament, not an essential part of the document. What was relevant, indeed the substance of the Plan document, was the general philosophical discourse on planning and development. And this was the contribution of J.J. Anjaria. Nehru understood this, when the government decided to award Padma Shri to Anjaria for his First Plan; but he deserved at least a Padma Vibhushan. The titles have been vulgarised because of the politics that now govern India.

To return to my theme, my education in economics. Apart from Anjaria and in some respects the lectures by B.V. Krishnamurthy, I did not learn much from others. Dr. Lakdawala's lectures on Public Finance had a lot of substance but the way in which he delivered his lectures—with up and down rhythm—made me drowsy. Professor Samant, who had taught us at the S.L.D. Arts College and was now at the School, taught us Business Cycles. I wondered whether he had a good grasp of the subject and his halting delivery could not make me very attentive. However, he did introduce us to Schumpeter's *Business Cycles,* which had just come to India. I profited much from reading Haberler's *Prosperity and Depression* and Schumpeter's *Business Cycles,* which introduced me to thinking about themes that were not discussed in mainstream economic teaching.

Being bored with lectures, I merely put in the attendance necessary for lectures at the School and then with a trunk full of books left for home at Ahmedabad for study. I just returned for the examinations and did well in all the papers. Then I asked Dr. Lakdawala whether one could expect a first class; he was quite pessimistic and said nobody so far had got it. But Professor Vakil said that it was not difficult for a good student to get a first class. So with some hope I returned to Ahmedabad.

Quite unexpectedly, my friend H.N. Pathak called on me at Ahmedabad and gave me a message from Professor Vakil that I had got a first class first and that he would like me to study for Ph.D. at the School. Professor Vakil had an affectionate regard for good students and was eager to help them from whichever part of India they came. He supported and encouraged Brahmananda, B.V. Krishnamurthy, K.S. Krishnaswami and many others.

I was awarded a K.T. Telang gold medal and William Wederburn and other scholarships. So when I rejoined the School, I was financially very comfortable. So I lazed around, wrote a note on my proposed thesis—Theory of Economic Policy, a pretentious and complex theme—and engaged in various other activities. At this time at the University Hall there was to be a debate on linguistic provinces. I was deputed by the School to open the debate and argue against linguistic provinces, which I thought would encourage linguistic nationalism and disrupt the unity of India. The chairman of the debate was M.C. Chagla, the Vice-Chancellor of Bombay University. My opponent was no other than a redoubtable K.M. Munshi, an eminent and shrewd politician and a lawyer of great eminence. A famous novelist in Gujarati and an exponent of Indian culture, he started the Bharatiya Vidya Bhavan. As a Congressman, he had consistently supported linguistic provinces. But I did get good support for my well-argued thesis. That led Professor Vakil to recruit me to work on Keeping Bombay as an Autonomous Unit with a group sponsored by K.M. Munshi, Indian Merchants' Chamber and supported by Professor Vakil and C.L. Gheewala, who was earlier my teacher at the S.L.D. Arts College and had introduced me with great eloquence and scholarship to Laski's *Grammar of Politics*. So I worked with Gheewala and prepared a well-argued case for Keeping Bombay out of Linguistic Politics. I also published in the *Times of India* a well-argued paper against linguistic provinces. This paper was liked by independent thinkers not attached to the Congress and was appreciated by Professor Vakil, K.M. Munshi and Gheewala.

After this, I studied for the competitive examination for the Indian Administrative Service (IAS), just to while away the time. Brahmananda, Gouri and I appeared for this examination in 1948. Meanwhile I had applied for admission to Harvard University for my Ph.D. course; my brother B.V. Bhatt was studying for an MBA at the Harvard Business School and was eager that I joined Harvard. He canvassed for me at Harvard, met Professor Bourbank, head of the faculty of Economics, and Professor Alwin Hansen. He told them about the reputation of the Bombay School, the only school of this type at that time, and about my obtaining a Master's degree in Economics with great honours. Professor Hansen was very favourable but told my brother that I should not be so ambitious as to work on my thesis Theory of Economic Policy but to take up a more manageable theme. And so I was admitted to Harvard and was to stay at Business School Hall (with a sitting-reading room and bedroom) with my brother.

On the boat to London, which was taking a large number of Indian students, I was informed of my selection for Indian Foreign Service (IFS). I was ranked fourth in the competitive examination and was to attend Oxford for my training. At London, Krishna Menon met me and asked me to be prepared to join Oxford after my medical examination. I had only two days at London before I took the plane to USA; he told me to delay my departure. I was not willing to do so partly because I was keen on an academic career and also because I was not sure of passing the medical examination because of my eyesight. Krishna Menon hurriedly organised my medical examination and I could depart for Harvard. A month after reaching Harvard, I received a letter from the Indian High Commission at London that I did not pass the medical examination because of my eyesight. The number of my glasses, being about five, was not a sign of poor eyesight, but this was a measure adopted by the British before independence and was not changed by the Government of India.

Though not keen on joining the IFS I did want to make a point that the rules adopted by the British for a type of service—the Indian Civil Service (ICS)—which probably required going on horseback in the district, was not appropriate for independent India. I wrote a letter from Harvard to Prime Minister Nehru to change such rules that did not affect members of the IAS in performing their duties. I did not get any reply because he did not get my letter in the first place; the Indian civil servants did not want him to receive it.

Just before leaving for Harvard, we learnt about Nathuram Godse's shooting of Gandhiji on 30 January 1948. The entire nation was shocked. He worked all his life for the social-cultural-economic development of his country and had been mentally, physically, and intellectually as active as ever. As Nehru noted in his memorable speech, "The light has gone out for us, but I am wrong for the light that shone in India still shall shine for a thousand years to come." For a long time thereafter I fasted on the 30th of every month in memory of this sad event. I wrote a piece in Gujarati on the universal message of the Mahatma in a well-known journal. All of Gandhiji's relations and friends and followers liked this article, including his niece Manubehn Gandhi, who was with him at the shooting. I liked her reminiscences and met her several times later on.

Several friends asked me why I had decided to go to Harvard instead of Cambridge, Oxford or the London School of Economics. All the well-known economists in India had gone to these institutions. For example, J.V. Joshi (who later became Executive Director at the Reserve Bank), L.K. Jha (the eminent ICS and later Governor of the Reserve Bank) and I.G. Patel studied at Cambridge and were also students of Keynes. Some others like H.T. Parekh (later on Chairman of ICICI), R.S. Bhatt (later on Chairman of the Unit Trust of India), the eminent economist A.K. Dasgupta and one of the ablest ICS, B.K. Nehru went to the London School. There were others like B.R. Shenoy and Professor Anjaria, who also studied at the London School.

After the war, A.G. Chandrasekhar and K.S. Krishnaswami also went to the London School.

I chose Harvard because of the eminent economists at Harvard—Schumpeter whose books I had read and was impressed by his brilliance and somewhat unorthodox style; Professor Hansen, whose books I had read; Chamberlain, whose book on monopolistic competition we studied at the Bombay School; and the presence at nearby MIT of Paul Samuelson, Resenstein Rodan and Rostow.

The other decisive factor was my brother, B.V. Bhatt, who was studying at Harvard Business School. He was keen that I should join him at Harvard and tried hard to get me admission at Harvard; at this time the Bombay School was not known to Harvard and my brother had to convince them of the significance of studies at the Bombay School.

And so, I chose Harvard without any hesitation or regrets.

At Harvard I was studying hard. The faculty was unsurpassed anywhere—Schumpeter, Leontief, Hansen, Haberler, Gerschenkron, Dussenbury and Carl Keysen. (A year later I worked as a teaching fellow with Dussenbury and Carl Keysen.) Richard Goodwin became a friend and we met along with his wife quite often. My brother knew him and he was very helpful to us during our stay at Harvard as well as in our academic pursuits.

Leontief taught Advanced Economic Theory. He was a good teacher, who made the subject interesting and easy to understand. In India, teachers taught books—Hicks, Joan Robinson, Chamberlain, etc. At Harvard the subject was more relevant than the individual books.

Schumpeter taught a specially advanced course on economic theory. He took up special themes and discussed them with great elegance and conviction. He would walk on the stage, and at various points take out a yellow slip to record a new thought that occurred to him while teaching. He never referred to his own theories or recommended his books. He was accessible to students and would discuss any themes that interested them, when they met him in his office. Even on the campus, he would hail any student even from a distance. In one of my sessions with him we were discussing Hayek. He simply asked me, why should his theory not lead to inflation rather than a recession. He urged me to think it through. He would give general lectures in the evening for all students. In one such lecture, he mentioned that all leaders are liars and Keynes was a great leader. It was quite amusing. At the end of the first semester, I went to him with my brother to take his photograph. He said, why not wait till I return for the next semester? He was preparing his lecture on March Towards Socialism for the American Economic Association. He never returned. Leontief gave a lecture on him, mentioning that he attained maturity much before he was 30 and attained his great reputation, while Keynes' success came to him when he was 55. It was Schumpeter's thesis that scientists get their original ideas before they are 30 and later on simply work on them. His essay on Keynes also showed that his original ideas were evolved much earlier than his *General Theory*.

On monetary-banking theory, we had lectures by John Williams and Hansen. Williams was present at the discussion on Bretton Woods institutions and from his firsthand knowledge informed us about the trend of the discussions. He gave us a long reading list. I was not sure whether one could read all of the books he mentioned. I asked him whether he wanted us to read all of them. He laughed and with good humour said, "read whatever you like." Hansen had just written his book on *Monetary Theory*. However, I did not learn much from all these lectures, as I already had read the relevant books.

With Haberler, I took a reading course on Business Cycles, partly to save on time for other subjects and partly because Haberler was not a good lecturer. At our sessions, he asked me what I had read. I told him that I had already read his book, Schumpeter's *Business Cycles* and the recent book by Hicks on *Trade Cycle*. He thought I had read enough and urged me to think about them. He was very kind. But when we discussed Indian poverty, he could not understand this phenomenon. Surprisingly for me he said, "Wasn't a Brahmin more important for India than the poverty-stricken masses?" I was aghast at this observation which ridiculed the uneducated, illiterate, depressed sections of humanity. At this stage even at Harvard there was not much appreciation of the Indian struggle for eliminating poverty. There was not much interest in the economic development of poor countries, except at MIT where Rosenstein Rodan and Rostow were engaged in research on development of the East European countries.

The most interesting and illuminating lectures on Economic History were by Alexander Gerschenkron. His style was to involve all students in discussion of the questions he was raising, so one had not only to listen but also to think of the questions at the same time. He was analysing the pattern of European history since 1776 and was comparing the English experience with industrial development with other latecomer European countries like France, Germany, Austria and Russia. His organising principle was the impact of economic backwardness on the countries that industrialised after England. Marx and later Rostow had argued that the late developing countries would imitate the experience of the UK; Gerschenkron's thesis was that the economically backward countries followed a different pattern—industrialisation spurt with high rates of growth based on steel-based heavy industries, the role of Universal Banks in initiating the process in less backward countries like France, Germany and Austria, and of the state in Russia (a more backward country) and a radical socialist ideology motivating the Universal Banks and the state (Russia) for generating a process of capitalist development. I was impressed by his thesis and thought that the Indian experience would be similar to the late developing European countries.

In answering a question he had raised for our examination, I quoted Wordsworth, "Bliss was in that dawn to be alive/But to be young was very Heaven." (I used to answer all questions before the allotted time and spend the rest of the time in embellishing my answers with apt quotations.) When I met him for my term papers, he recognised me (I had not met him earlier) as one who had quoted Wordsworth. He was an erudite scholar of not only economic history but also of literature (and in particular Russian literature). On Nobokov's English translation of Pushkin, he made critical comments and suggested revisions that only a scholar of his eminence could make.

On my term paper, I had thought of the British industrialisation experience in the nineteenth century. The first paper was to be on the first part of the nineteenth century and the second paper (for the next term) on late nineteenth century. He said that I should not rely exclusively on Rostow's book but should consult other sources. I agreed and said that I would rather discuss the Long Cycle hypothesis (of Kondrieff) as presented by Schumpeter in his Business Cycles. Needless to say, he appreciated my term papers with his usual generosity.

At this time Pandit Nehru visited the United States. There was great praise in the media and elsewhere for this great leader from

India. The US government expected him to accept a military pact with the USA. Once he declined to do so and to change his foreign policy of neutrality with regard to the Great Powers—Russia and the USA—the mood in the USA changed against him. He addressed Indian students at the MIT auditorium and explained his stance on foreign policy, which he declared was consistent with India's recent history and the principles of Gandhiji. When he was leaving the stage, my brother took my photograph with him. He, with great grace and with the love for Indian students, stopped for a moment at my brother's request.

I had decided to appear for the oral examination required before starting my Ph.D. thesis. All my friends advised me not to appear for this difficult examination just before one year. Normally, students took two years before appearing for this examination. Anyway, because of financial constraints and my feeling that I would pass this examination, I decided to appear for it, even before my second semester's written examinations.

My examiners were my teachers—Leontief, Hansen, Haberler and Gerschenkron. Feeling that I was nervous Gerschenkron got up to shake my hand and offered a cigarette, a gesture I appreciated. Anyway, I did reasonably well—except for my inability to answer some questions. I felt that I would not fail in this examination. But to my great surprise, after only half an hour, Leontief came to me and said that they had decided to give me the highest grade, excellent. My brother and I felt very pleased with this unexpected result and all my friends came to congratulate me.

Professor Hansen was so pleased with me that he took me immediately to Arthur Smithies (Dean of the Faculty) and requested him with great fervour to grant me a teaching fellowship for 1951-52. For the year 1950-51, the decisions were already taken. Thus, it became possible to come to Harvard in 1951.

I got my Master's degree at the same time that my brother got his MBA and both of us returned home by June 1950. I was offered a teaching job at my own college, S.L.D. Arts College. Thus for one year, before going to Harvard, I taught Economics to B.A. students, while my brother rejoined his college, H.L. College of Commerce, as a teacher in Modern Economic Development.

My school friend Probodh Pandit (after getting a Ph.D. from London) was teaching Sanskrit at my college. My one-time teacher D.N. Pathak was teaching Politics. Niranjan Bhagat, another friend (who was junior to me by two years at the Navchetan High School), a poet of great reputation, was teaching Gujarati Literature. There were also my old teachers—S.R. Bhatt (teaching English Literature) and A.G. Bhatt and Athwalae (teaching Sanskrit). So it was a friendly environment. I spent a pleasant year in their company.

At this time the government took a decision to start Gujarat University. Pandit and Pathak, like me, were eager to see that this university would be as good as Harvard or British universities. We were prepared to work for such a university.

When the decisions were to be taken to appoint the vice-chancellor and members of the governing council, we decided to write about the shape such a university should take. We published a booklet on this theme, which was reproduced in several well-known journals—*Shikshan ann Sahitya, Jyotirdhar ann Sanskriti*. We personally delivered this booklet to all who were to take decisions about the vice-chancellor and members of the governing council.

In September 1951, I returned to Harvard to complete my Ph.D. dissertation. I had to take a course in Statistics, taught by Orcut, to complete the requirements for the Ph.D. degree and at the same time work on my Ph.D. thesis. As a teaching fellow, I worked in the first semester with Professor Dussenbury (known for his research on saving behaviour) who had earlier analysed the role of demonstration effect on the behaviour of saving. In the second semester, I worked with Carl Keysen. Since I had to examine the answers to their question papers, I had also to attend their lectures. Keysen urged me to take some sessions on the contribution of Harrod-Domar, which I did and the students liked my lectures. Earlier Dussenbury thought American students would not understand my language; hence he did not urge me to take a few lectures. Keysen knew that I was good at English; hence he wanted me to take a few sessions.

For the theme of my thesis, I had only a vague idea of what I would like to do. It had to be relevant for India's problems. I knew that, as Gandhiji said, poverty cannot be diminished without providing productive employment to the unemployed and the underemployed; but this was not possible without generating a process of economic development, as argued by Nehru. Thus, I wanted to work on a theme that would be relevant for employment and economic development of poor countries, and in particular India.

With these thoughts I met Gerschenkron and Leontief. Gerschenkron had just got the census of manufacturing industries in India. He gave that to me and said it might be useful in examining how Indian industries choose their technology. Leontief was working on capital coefficients at this time. He advised me that one should take a theme which is relevant for understanding a certain economic phenomenon in which one is interested. Only then, he said, one can make a scientific contribution. He was not in favour of mere abstract—but irrelevant—theorising.

So I started working with Leontief as my adviser on the theme of choice of technology and techniques, based on empirical data, by modern industries in India and other developing countries. On the basis of their resource endowments one would expect that they would choose less capital-intensive technology compared to similar industries in developed countries. So I got absorbed in collecting data (not often readily available, from various sources), including from correspondence with various firms in India and elsewhere. This turned out to be a time-consuming process. But the written responses from firms and the industrial associations were very useful as they explained why they chose certain technologies and techniques.

I completed my first preliminary draft, which showed that capital-output ratios in developing countries were more or less similar to what they were in developed countries. Leontief urged me to collect data on capital-labour ratios or on capital intensity in developing countries. So again one had to correspond with industrial firms, for gathering these data, which showed that developing countries did use much more labour-intensive techniques in certain processes like materials handling and some other processes than developed countries. Thus, it became clear that there is some choice with regard to technology and that production functions were not the same in developing countries as in developed countries. This also led me to find out whether such labour-intensive technologies were really available for developing countries. Thus two more chapters were added to my preliminary draft and their implications for the process of economic development. Thus my first chapter was on choice of techniques, and the other on its implications for the rate of growth of income and employment. But, as I learnt from Gerschenkron, the development process would require initiative from development-oriented state policies for creating an environment favourable for private sector entrepreneurial functioning in relatively backward countries. So I outlined some elements of development strategy for developing countries on the basis of the historical experience of developed countries at the time of their initial stage of industrialisation and current experience of some developing countries like India. These were: the state-initiated process of planned development; the role of the state in creating a favourable environment for private entrepreneurial talents for introducing innovations; choice of investment pattern based on the development of steel and steel-based basic industries in countries like India on the basis of their dynamic comparative advantage; modernising through technical and organisational innovation; the labour-intensive cottage and small-scale industries, producing entire consumption goods; emphasis on innovative techniques for promoting agricultural development.

On this basis, I outlined an aggregative planning model based on Harrod-Domar equation, which indicated the requirement for increasing the saving-income ratio to attain the desired rate of growth of economy once the capital-output ratio was estimated on the basis of the chosen investment pattern.

Some elements of this strategy were incorporated in the Second Five Year Plan. However, the Plan emphasised the development of basic industries on the basis of an article of faith—machine to make machines—rather than on dynamic comparative advantage, which was consistent with taking advantage of foreign trade. Secondly, instead of trying to create a favourable environment for the entrepreneurial functioning in the private sector, it relied on licences and controls that stifled entrepreneurial functioning. In its planning model, it failed to take account of the inflow of foreign resources—through external assistance and transfer of foreign resources—for raising the investment-income ratio. So the result has been that India failed to realise its potential for development, till 1990, because of certain negative processes, inimical to the vigorous functioning of private enterprise.

I submitted my thesis for Ph.D., approved by Leontief and his colleagues. At this time, a distinguished economist—Hans Singer, visited Harvard; he was in charge of research on development of poor countries at the United Nations. He approached Haberler to suggest a person to do research at the United Nations. Haberler suggested my name and arranged for an interview with him. However, I had decided to go back to India to participate in some small measure in its development process. So I declined this offer as well as others from the IMF and desired to return to India, after my Ph.D.

In that year I made good friends. Muzamil Haque was from Pakistan. He later on joined ECAFE in Bangkok and then returned to Bangladesh. He was a great admirer of Tagore and was also in love with a Hindu girl in Bangladesh. This did not materialise for religious reasons and he married an American. I met them in Bangkok, when he was working at ECAFE in 1955. Nurul Islam, another friend, later on worked in Pakistan, Bangladesh and the International Food Research Institute. Tun Thin, from Burma, later on joined the IMF. Subimal Mukerjee also became my friend during this time.

I returned to India in January 1952 and rejoined the S.L.D. Arts College. The dream of a University of Gujarat did not materialise because of politics intruding with educational institutions. So I joined the research department of the Reserve Bank of India in April 1953. This decision, in retrospect, was a wise one as I matured as a development economist because of the work I did—partly on my initiative and partly because of research required at this institution. My later work as an economist was largely determined by my involvement in the research that was required not only for the Reserve Bank but also for the themes that were relevant for the Reserve Bank as well as the government in areas relevant for development and planning. The Reserve Bank provided me with a favourable environment for initiating research on the themes I liked and were at the same time relevant for development policies. But more on this in the next chapter.

While at Harvard I met Martin Luther King with a friend of mine. He was at that time having reading sessions on the autobiography of Mahatma Gandhi. Since they came to know of my own interest in Gandhiji's *satyagraha* technique, I was invited to attend their reading sessions and discuss some aspects of Gandhiji's life. For the same reasons, I met the members of the organisations dedicated to racial equality in New York.

In my first semester, P.N. Dhar had come to work with Leontief. We became friends. He came from Kashmir and was anxiously concerned about the developments there. He spoke about these problems whenever we met. Later on, he became Director of Indian Institute of Economic Growth and later worked as Adviser to Prime Minister Indira Gandhi. He played some crucial role in persuading Mrs. Gandhi to lift the emergency that she had declared and organise parliamentary elections. After Mrs. Gandhi lost the election in 1976-1977, Dhar worked at the World Bank as a consultant and we renewed our friendship.

Harvard taught me to collect data from disparate sources, and put them together in a meaningful way for the analysis of different problems. This Leontief mentioned as scientific work, relevant for understanding economic phenomena. He did not approve of mere abstract theoretical work that did not relate to the understanding of the working of an economic system.

I did not realise then that I was the first Indian Ph.D. in Economics from Harvard after the World War. I was followed by Subimal Mukerjee, a friend from Assam, Muzamil Haque and Nurul Islam from Pakistan and Tun Thin from Burma. I.G. Patel had spent a year before I joined Harvard but at that time I did not know about him at Harvard. He gathered some data at Harvard for his thesis for which he got a Ph.D. from Cambridge University in the U.K. Maybe our presence at Harvard encouraged Harvard to understand the economic problems of developing countries as well as the work of the MIT team on developing countries, particularly India, when India initiated a process of planned economic development.

3

At the Reserve Bank of India (1953–1972)

Reserve Bank's first Indian Governor, C.D. Deshmukh, was highly imaginative and far-sighted in understanding the importance of economic analysis and policy for planned economic development. He had a Cambridge degree in Botany and later passed the ICS examination; he had a distinguished career as a member of the ICS. Later he joined the Reserve Bank of India as Deputy Governor and after independence became the first Indian Governor. Apart from his scientific training and enormous experience in government, he was a great Sanskrit scholar.

Since he realised the importance of economic research and economists, he started strengthening the Department of Research and Statistics by employing young and promising economists not only for the current work at the Reserve Bank but also for future work in the Bank and in the government, relating to the planned process of development that was initiated after India became a republic. He already had his good senior economists—J.V. Joshi (a star pupil of Keynes and later a Cambridge graduate in Economics and distinguished member of the economic team in the government) as Executive Director in charge of research and a highly reputed and experienced economist—Dr. B.K. Madan—as Economic Adviser. All three of them were responsible for the recruitment of highly qualified young economists. Young economists, many of them educated at Cambridge, Oxford, London School and Harvard, were also eager to join the prestigious Research Department.

The process of selection was rigorous. When I applied for a position in the Research Department, eighteen economists were interviewed for selection. The first interview was with J.V. Joshi and the Economic Adviser (at that time Narayan Prasad. The second interview was with the Governor—Sir Benegal Rama Rao—and the Deputy Governors. At the Governor's interview, I was brash in answering some question by the Deputy Governor—Sundereshan—that put him in a tight corner. Rama Rao was amused and gave a benign smile as Sundereshan did not quite respond to my answer.

I was selected for the position of a Research Officer along with A.G. Chandavarkar, who had a degree with high honours from the London School of Economics. Later, Joshi smilingly told me that I was at a university started by a Cambridge graduate and that Chandavarkar was a student when the London School was cooperating with Cambridge. Joshi was at Cambridge and was taught by Keynes and hence he liked candidates associated with Cambridge in some way. I was the first to be recruited from an American university—Harvard. Chandavarkar and I became good friends. He had also studied at the Bombay School. At that time I was a paying guest at a Premchand Lalchand house near Chaupatty and Chandavarkar with his wife Tara was staying at Gamdevi. We would walk after work along Marine Drive and I often stayed with them for dinner. He had written an article in the *Economics Journal* on the limitations of savings potential, as discussed by Nurkse. So there were common topics to discuss with him, as has been the case since then and even now in Washington.

Deshmukh's imaginative strengthening of the Department of Research and Statistics made it possible for the Government of India to staff the Ministry of Finance as well as the Planning Commission. Prof. J.I. Anjaria was deputed to become the Chief Economic Adviser to the Ministry of Finance and Planning Commission. K.N. Raj and Krishnaswami were deputed to the Planning Commission to finalise the First Five Year Plan. V.K. Ramaswami went to the Ministry of Finance (he later became Chief Economic Adviser). The Industrial Development Bank of India and Unit Trust of India (both owned by the Reserve Bank of India) had their economists from the Reserve Bank.

The Reserve Bank is known for meticulous collection, analysis and dissemination of data on various aspects of the Indian economy. These are published in its Currency and Finance reports. The Ministry of Finance, Planning Commission and economists engaged in research on India's problems and policies rely on these data. This had been possible because of the talented staff of economists and statisticians recruited by Deshmukh and his successors. It is somewhat surprising that even the Government of India did not appreciate and acknowledge its reliance on the data published by the Reserve Bank. Only Professor Anjaria recognised the importance of Reserve Bank data. Whenever we went to Delhi for discussion with him relating to various aspects of economic policies, he always relied on our data rather than the data furnished by his staff. It is amazing that I.G. Patel, who relied on Reserve Bank data submitted to him by his staff, did not even mention how useful these data were in his memoirs on economic policy; and not even a word about the research done in the Reserve Bank and published in its Bulletins. Since Anjaria was head of the Division of Monetary Economics at the Reserve Bank, which was coordinating all the material for publication in Currency and Finance and Reserve Bank Bulletins, he was well aware of the significance of these publications. Hence he respected the researchers at the Reserve Bank, unlike his staff.

Initially, I was put in the Balance of Payments Division, with Pendarkar as the Director. I learnt at first the methodology of the compiling of the data on balance of payments and later on wrote a booklet along with my colleague Kumarasundaram (who later worked with the ICICI) on the trends in India's balance of payments and the way in which we compiled the data. Pendarkar was very active in improving the data as well as in educating his staff in the field of balance of payments. He arranged for these classes for education in the evening after work and urged me to take a few sessions, based on Meade's book on the subject. Pendarkar had a degree in Statistics from London University and he had considerable experience in compiling data and analysis based on them. He made the division a vibrant part of the Research Department. But soon after, he left as an Alternative Executive Director at the IMF, along with Narayan Prasad.

Meanwhile, to my great surprise, the *Review of Economics and Statistics* (a Harvard journal) invited me (probably at the instance of Leontief) to present the chapter in my thesis on the "Comparative

Capital Coefficients of Developed and Developing Countries" for publication. I had no idea or ambition of publishing any part of my thesis but submitted the chapter as requested. This was published in the issue of August 1954, much sooner than I had expected. This was the second article in an international journal of repute by an Indian economist (the first was by R.C. Desai in 1947) and several of my friends noticed it with some pride.

Since then, having acquired some confidence in my findings, I published my third chapter on "Capital Intensity in Developing and Developed Countries" in the Oxford University's *Bulletin of Statistics* in May 1956, and my fourth chapter on "Employment and Capital Formation" in *Economia Internazionale* in February 1958. The other three chapters were published in the *Indian Economic Journal* (July 1953, October 1954 and July 1957). My articles in the *Review of Economics and Statistics* and in Oxford Bulletin were mentioned by Tinbergen as required reading by the economic staff of the ECAFE.

Later on I worked on "Criteria for Choice of Techniques" and published this article in the *Economic Journal* (June 1958).

One part of my chapter, which discussed the potential for employment generation by modernising through technology research, the cottage and traditional small-scale industries, was published in *Economic Weekly* in Octpber 1954.

All these articles, related to my thesis, were published as a book—*Employment and Capital Formation in Underdeveloped Economies*—in September 1960 (Orient Longman). I should have published this work—which had anticipated the discussion that took place in the 1950s with regard to the development problems of India and the other developing countries—earlier, were it not for my laziness and absorption in the research work at the Reserve Bank.

My tentative findings on capital coefficients in developing and developed countries, which were published in the *Review of Economics and Statistics* in August 1954 were found to be valid even in the light of much more data that became available later on by Young Chin Kim in his article in the same journal (in its issue in 1969). To quote: "The present study not only confirms his earlier findings on the basis of more comprehensive data ..."

Moreover, Ezekiel of the *Economic Times*, in his review of my book noted that all the main elements of development strategy of the Second Five Year Plan were anticipated in my work done in 1951-52. He has been a well-known economist, having got his Ph.D. from the Bombay School of Economics, where later on he taught Economics. His commentaries on India's economic policies and significant current developments in his column in the *Economic Times* were avidly read by economists because of his informed and erudite discussion of their impact on Indian economic development. He was also a critic of the development strategy adopted in the Second Five Year Plan. Later on he worked with the IMF, where he was highly regarded for his expertise.

Just a few months after I joined the Reserve Bank I had a telephone call from the eminent, imaginative and farsighted editor—Sachin Choudhri—of the *Economic Weekly* to meet him at his dilapidated office. I remembered that I had met him in the later half of 1948, a few months after he started his *Weekly*. My colleagues and I had written four papers on the analysis of inflation in India. B.V. Krishnamurthy liked these papers—he was then teaching at the Bombay School—and suggested that we should publish them in the *Economic Weekly*. So he arranged for an interview with Sachin—who relied on him for contributions to his weekly. I found Sachin to be a *pan*-chewing person, with thick glasses and hoarse voice. He asked me several questions about our papers, which I thought were irrelevant and did not evince his knowledge of economics. Having acquired a Master's degree in the entire subject of Economics at the prestigious Bombay School, which was then the only school of its type in India, we were at that time a little arrogant. So we refused to submit our papers in his weekly. They were published in the *Journal of the Bombay University*.

Five years had elapsed since then, and after talking to various friends and Sachin himself I found what a significant role the *Weekly* played in India for inspiring and encouraging young economists to think and write on various themes relevant for India's economic development. It had become a medium for discussion and debate about various aspects of socioeconomic policies and economic development and strategy. He encouraged all economists to write in this *Weekly*, irrespective of their ideology as long as these articles contributed to vigorous discussion, which can enlighten those who were interested in serious discussion of India's policies. He had no ideological bias and cultivated all young economists who could contribute to his *Weekly*, which had the motto: Light Without Heat. He had a knack of locating promising young economists. Having learned about me possibly from my friends like K.S. Krishnaswamy, he thought that I could be useful in strengthening the *Weekly*. And so we met. Since then I have had a lifelong friendship with him and his *Weekly* and later on had a significant association with Hazari and Krishna Raj, who were editors of the new incarnation of the *Weekly*—*Economic and Political Weekly*. Krishna Raj made *EPW* much more relevant for the themes of not only socioeconomic development but also politics, history and several other themes that can contribute to knowledge and enlightenment.

I wrote for the *Weekly* initially anonymously and later as Savya Sachi, a pseudonym suggested by Sachin. Sometimes he would call on me at short notice to comment on recent events and sometimes for writing editorials. On my own, I wrote several articles anonymously or as Savya Sachi. The *Economic Weekly* was unique in combining editorial comments, notes and comments on recent events and, above all, learned articles on various themes by Indian and foreign economists.

My first piece was a critical comment on an article by K.N. Raj, a friend of Sachin and strong supporter of the *Weekly*. This comment later on in the discussion was referred to as by a person called X. Immediately after this, I wrote a satirical piece (authored by Y, as the discussants called the author) on Raj's citing authorities in support of his thesis. I described this method of discussion as being in *Shastric* tradition). This discussion and debate continued for some time. Later Joan Robinson summed up the discussion in an article.

K.N. Raj did not like my comments, Sachin told me, and complained why he published such nonsense. While telling me this he was having a hearty laugh. He said that the *Weekly* did not respect any authority (including that of its friends and supporters). This was the first time a controversy was generated in the *Weekly*.

Immediately after, another controversy commenced. Amartya Sen had written an article in the *Weekly* on the opportunity cost of labour in India. This provoked one "Shrinivasan" (pseudonym for Deena Khatkhate) to make critical comments on the article. This controversy went on for some time. Sachin, who liked Sen as a promising young economist and as a friend, was not deterred from publishing "Shrinivasan's" several rejoinders. (I met Sen in 1965 in Bangkok where I was working as a development economist at the United Nations' Asian Institute of Economic Development and Planning. When he was invited as an economist he asked me in a very friendly way who were "X", "Y" and "Shrinivasan". We had a hearty laugh after I disclosed their identity.)

The third controversy, for which I was responsible, arose as a result of Jagdish Bhagwati's article, which he had sent for publication in the *Weekly*. The entire Delhi establishment—I.G. Patel, K.N. Raj and the rest—and A.K. Dasgupta, a highly respected friend of Sachin, a supporter of the *Weekly* and an eminent economist—were all against any public discussion of such a sensitive issue as the devaluation of the rupee. Sachin was pondering about publishing Jagdish's well-argued piece. When we met, as we did frequently at his Churchill Chambers flat, he asked my view. I said, "Sachin, your motto is Light Without Heat. You pride yourself as an editor who wants to generate free discussion and debate. How can you not publish this well-reasoned article by a young promising economist?" Sachin saw my point and published the article, which generated a lively controversy, initially after a rejoinder by A.K. Dasgupta, who was against rupee devaluation.

Such, then, had been the *Economic Weekly* and has been its later incarnation—the *Economic and Political Weekly*.

I must cite one other instance that illustrates Sachin's devotion to adhere to his motto of Light Without Heat. Pitambar Pant was then working on the dimension of the Second Five Year Plan in his Division of Perspective Planning of the Planning Commission. That was a time when a sort of consensus was generated among the Planning Commission, young Indian economists, and also supported by eminent foreign economists about a plan that would emphasise the development of basic industries—machine to make machines—as indicated by the Mahalanobis approach. Sachin asked me to write an editorial commenting on the way in which planning was taking place. I wrote a very critical editorial, emphasising the crudity of the planning process, which neglected the implications of the strategy for inter-sector development and its disregard for the constraints of domestic and foreign resources. The editorial was titled "Platitudes on Planning", which Sachin published without any changes. Pitambar was annoyed by such a piece and wrote to Sachin complaining about such destructive critique of the planning process. Sachin as usual disregarded this complaint, in spite of his close relation with Pitambar Pant.

I explained the logic of my criticism by writing an article on input-output technique as tool for planning in a later issue of the *Weekly*. At this time Richard Goodwin was in India, as a consultant to the Ministry of Finance and Planning Commission. When he came to the Bombay School of Economics, he read my article and said, "I could not have written on this technique better than you have done." I knew Goodwin from my Harvard days. Among all the foreign economists that came to India at this time at the invitation of Mahalanobis, Goodwin's contribution to the planning process was most significant. The other economist who commented on Indian planning and development in a very creative and constructive manner was Gunnar Myrdal, who wrote his book *Asian Drama* in India, while he was in Delhi along with his wife Alva Myrdal, whose research with regard to the impact of education for Indian development was published in a chapter on education in Gunnar's book.

From 1966, I wrote all my articles in my name, beginning with one on external assistance. This was the article Sachin was reading when he passed away. It was later published in the first issue of the *Economic and Political Weekly*, and later was brought out by it as a pamphlet.

My important work in the Reserve Bank started after 1955, after I got married in January 1955 to Prafulla Dave—who had her Bachelor's degree in Sanskrit. After marriage she obtained Master's degree in Sociology from the Bombay School of Economics and Sociology. She has been helping me since then in my work in various significant ways, as have been my daughters, Swati, Gita and Shuchi.

After two years of work on balance of payments, I was deputed by the Reserve Bank to participate in a seminar for young economists organised by the International Economic Association and the Bombay School of Economics with Prof. C.N. Vakil, taking charge of administration details. This was a welcome break to acquaint myself with recent works on economic development.

The international economists who initiated discussion at the seminar were Joan Robinson, Nicholas Kaldor, Downie—all from the UK—and Tarshis from Canada. D.R. Gadgil and V.K.R.V. Rao were from India. I may just mention a few highlights.

Robinson had just completed her book on *Accumulation of Capital*—a title which she liked as that was the title of the well-known book by Rosa Luxemburg. She discussed the themes on economic growth as she presented in her book. She related these themes to Indian planning process. This evoked considerable discussion.

Kaldor had just completed his book on *Expenditure Tax* and he discussed why he thought this was the best tax from the point of view of promoting savings required for economic development. He also maintained that the really relevant part of Economics were theories related to macroeconomics. I intervened to observe that innovations are invariably carried out in a few significant sectors and hence aggregative analysis cannot capture this process of technological change; this I had learnt from Schumpeter. My comment induced Robinson to argue vigorously for my point of view and made critical comments on Kaldor's thesis. This was one of the most exciting sessions. As usual, Kaldor very calmly defended his position with great clarity and lucidity.

At lunch Kaldor always joined us and we had good discussion on various themes, including the relevance of Keynes and Schumpeter. I mentioned that however important Schumpeter's theory was, his method of exposition was much more descriptive than analytical. Kaldor immediately endorsed my view with his lucid exposition of the contribution of Schumpeter, which he greatly admired.

At one point at our lunch discussions he made some observation on the 1857 revolt in India and I was constrained to comment that his generalisation was based on ignorance. He was taken aback at my brash comment but Robinson enjoyed his discomfiture and was greatly amused.

There was one incident which was a little embarrassing for me and I should mention it. Since we were in Poona, I suggested that all the participants should take a break to visit Ellora and Ajanta, not very far from Poona. Robinson, Kaldor and the rest liked this idea. This suggestion was conveyed by B.V. Krishnamurthy (who was deputed by Professor Vakil to look after the administration of the seminar) to Professor Vakil, mentioning that Bhatt was responsible for this suggestion. Professor Vakil got very much annoyed with me for interfering in the affairs of the administration and conduct of the seminar by suggesting this trip, which was not part of the planning of the seminar. He told B.V. that Bhatt should not meddle in this planning of the seminar activities. However, since everybody wanted such a break, Professor Vakil had to comply despite the cost this trip involved. And so we went to Ellora and Ajanta.

For me, this seminar discussion helped in evolving an analytical framework to review the performance of an economy with regard to economic change and policies.

In the course of the seminar, Robinson and Kaldor visited Bombay and gave some lectures also at the Reserve Bank. Governor Benegal Rama Rao and senior officials of the Reserve Bank attended these lectures. At the end, Robinson and Kaldor mentioned to the Governor how they liked and appreciated my contribution at the seminar and mentioned that Bhatt was a star participant. Because of these observations by Robinson and Kaldor my reputation as a good young economist in the Reserve Bank got established. And a little later, the Governor asked me personally to prepare a significant paper, to be submitted directly to him. The paper was to be on the relative strength of the economies of the USA and the UK.

At that time, discussions were going on in the Ministry of Finance and Reserve Bank about the currency—dollar on sterling—in which Reserve Bank should keep its reserves and with which the rupee's value should be linked. I prepared a comprehensive analysis of past trends and future prospects of these two economies and concluded that the US economy was the stronger of the two with regard to stability and prospects for future growth.

I had to submit this paper directly to the Governor on 16 May. On that day there was a general strike of bank employees and Deena Khatkhate and I could not enter the office as the strikers blocked the entrance. So I made a telephone call to my research assistant, who had entered the office much before the demonstration by the strikers, and requested him to submit my paper directly to the Governor.

Next day an amusing incident happened. Reserve Bank administration under the Deputy Governor—Ambegaokar—asked all staff who had not attended the office to explain their absence. Both

Dina and I explained that the Reserve Bank should have made it possible to enter the office. Ambegaokar considered this explanation as an insult to the Reserve Bank and suggested to Dr. Pinto (who was then in charge of the Research Department) that these officers should be severely admonished. Dr. Pinto calmly argued that these were very responsible officers and did not deserve to be admonished as they were prevented by the strikers from entering. Ambegaokar finally relented. As a Deputy Governor he was impulsive and arrogant. He was an ICS officer before joining the Reserve Bank and some of such officers were used to giving commands and exercise these powers without any need to do so.

For another incident thereafter I thought I might be admonished. Dr. B.K. Madan (who was at that time Economic Adviser, and was responsible for strengthening the Research Department with his intelligence, erudition, tact and concern for all officers) took me along with him to attend the annual session of the Indian Economic Conference. At this venue, I suggested that the currency standard for India was inappropriate and should be changed to meet the requirement of currency expansion. I suggested that foreign exchange reserves were meant to be used for emergencies—*à la* Keynes—and should not govern currency expansion. Then I realised that Dr. Madan would admonish me for discussing sensitive issues of economic policy in a public forum. But to my surprise, after the end of the session, he came to me, put his hand on my shoulder and had his fascinating smile. I was relieved.

Then on my own initiative I worked on the impact of the suggested investment during the Second Five Year Plan and the recent import liberalisation on our foreign exchange reserves. My analysis showed that we should be prepared for a serious decline in our foreign exchange reserves. I submitted this paper to Ramanujam, who was the head of the Balance of Payments Division. He read the paper and said that my conclusion about the impact on foreign exchange reserves was not realistic as India in the past few years had not experienced any foreign exchange crisis. So he did not submit my paper to the Governor. Very soon, during the first half of the first year of the Second Plan, our reserves declined by a very large amount and India experienced a foreign exchange crisis. The Second Plan was formulated without any serious examination of its impact on foreign exchange reserves and even on domestic resources. There was a slogan that whatever was physically possible should also be financially viable. It was not examined through analysis of inter-sectoral balances by the use of input-output technique even for the feasibility of implementing the investment plan—as I had observed in my article ("Anonymous" in the *Economic Weekly*) and the financial implications were not even examined. Hence, the Plan had to be pruned, import control became rigorous and the era of obtaining external assistance, through the World Bank initiative of establishing a World Bank Aid India Consortium, started. All these created a mentality prone to licence-permit *raj* among government officials and the cabinet, with very serious adverse consequences for the growth of the economy for several years till almost 1991.

The Second Plan merely outlined a development strategy—state-initiated process of planning development with emphasis on steel-based basic industries. This was not a novel strategy; the National Planning Committee and the industrialists in the Bombay Plan had already advocated this strategy. Mahalanobis merely formalised with his model the same strategy; as he himself said, he had merely based his model on the ideas of Jawaharlal Nehru, who was earlier Chairman of the National Planning Committee. This distracted the attention of the economists, who merely indulged in such two-sector-four-sector models without tackling the substantive issues about the Plan. These issues related to the resources constraint—both domestic and external—for implementing investment requirements. It was assumed that deficit financing would fill the gap, if domestic resources were not adequate. Further, the planners did not estimate the overall and sectoral saving on a firmer basis. They relied on guesstimates about saving and investment in the Indian economy. They also did not have any idea about the income distribution pattern in the Indian economy. The Plan thus was based on wishful thinking with the slogan that what was physically possible should also be financially viable.

So in the Reserve Bank, we tried to do what the Planning Commission or Ministry of Finance had failed to undertake. The first problem we tried to tackle was to estimate the non-inflationary level of deficit financing. Deena Khatkhate and I started working on this theme. Milton Friedman was then in India and spent some time with us in the Reserve Bank. There was no other economist to match his rare expertise with regard to monetary matters. We had several discussions with him and he suggested that we should attempt an analysis of determinants of money supply. At the same time Dr. B.K. Madan, Economic Adviser at the Reserve Bank, suggested to us, knowing our interest and work on this theme, that we should undertake an analysis of money supply. For this purpose, he appointed a research committee comprising S.L.N. Sinha (Director, Monetary Economic Division) as chairman and A.G. Chandavarkar, Deena Khatkhate and me as members. I prepared the first draft of our report and this was discussed in our committee meetings. Finally we prepared two papers, one on analysis of money supply and the other on estimation of the level of non-inflationary deficit financing. It may be mentioned that B.R. Shenoy was the first economist who argued that the Second Plan would have to rely on the level of deficit financing that might be inflationary. No other economist raised this issue. Anyway, we attempted to estimate the non-inflationary level of deficit financing. These two papers were published in the *Reserve Bank Bulletin* (July, August 1961).

The second study I attempted related to the estimation of overall and sectoral saving. The editor (Hoselitz) of *Economic Development and Culture Change* intended to bring out a special issue on the Indian economy. He asked me to write an article on savings and capital formation in India. I developed the methodology for estimating saving and investment and this was published in the April 1959 issue of the journal.

Possibly because of my article, ECAFE requested the central banks of member countries (including India) to estimate saving and investment in their countries. Dr. B.K. Madan asked me to prepare these estimates. Now I had much more data than I had earlier. I tapped disparate sources of available data, making some plausible assumptions and prepared the first ever estimates of saving and investment. These papers were published in the *Reserve Bank Bulletin* (March 1960 and April 1961).

In 1960-61, there was vigorous discussion on the impact of development on income distribution in the Press as well as in Parliament. It was argued in public discussions that the degree of inequality had increased and the fruits of development had not reduced poverty in India. My colleague P.D. Ojha and I felt that it was time that we estimated the pattern of income distribution during

1953-54 and 1956-57. So we started this study on our own on the basis of disparate data from several sources and prepared a paper on "Distribution of Income in the Indian Economy." This was published in the *Reserve Bank Bulletin* (September 1962 and September 1963). Dr. Madan, who was a member of the Income Distribution Committee chaired by Mahalanobis and appointed by the Prime Minister, used these estimates in his discussion with members of the committee. He took me to a meeting of this committee to observe the tenor of discussion. In that meeting Mahalanobis argued that inequality of income distribution had been not only the result of income distribution but also due to the inequality of opportunities for education, as the latter is monopolised by the affluent classes. On the basis of this study, we published two papers—one in the *Bulletin of the Oxford University Institute of Economics and Statistics* (No. 3, 1964) and the other in the *American Economic Review* (September 1964). In these papers, we also attempted to estimate the extent of tax evasion that was taking place in India.

In 1962-63 there was considerable discussion in the Indian Press as well as in the United States on the impact of United States' commodity assistance to India on money supply. B.R. Shenoy argued in several articles in the Press and his letters to the World Bank as well as to members of the Unites States Congress that this assistance was financed by deficit financing, resulting in inflation in India. Dr. Madan asked me and Deena Khatkhate to examine this issue. We found that Shenoy's argument was not valid and that this assistance did not result in deficit financing. This paper was published in the *Reserve Bank Bulletin* (January 1963). Shenoy challenged our analysis in his articles in the *Economic Times*. This resulted in three or four articles by Shenoy and our rebuttal in the *Economic Times*. Dr. Ezekiel, who was in the *Economic Times* as an economist, summed up this controversy and supported our thesis, to Shenoy's chagrin. Later on, there was a high-power meeting, chaired by Gadgil and L.K. Jha, in Delhi to discuss this problem; V.G. Pendarkar and I attended this meeting. The result was not in favour of Shenoy's thesis.

It may be mentioned that our article in the *Reserve Bank Bulletin* was the result of our discussion with Pendarkar, who clearly pointed out the fallacy of the Shenoy argument.

Governor Iyengar was invited to give a lecture at the National Bank of Egypt. Under its auspices several well-known economists like

Sir Arthur Lewis and R.S. Sayers had delivered lectures earlier. Iyengar chose the theme "Development Strategy and Policies in India after Independence", in the light of economic change under British rule since 1800. I prepared extensive material for this lecture. However, later on the Governor decided to speak on monetary and fiscal policies. Meanwhile, Baroda University's Economics Department, chaired by my friend I.S. Gulati, invited me to give three lectures on the theme I had worked on for the Governor. I gave these lectures and they were published in my book *Aspects of Economic Change and Policy in India: 1800-1960* (Allied Publishers, Bombay, 1963). Earlier, based on this book, I published an article, "A Century and a Half of Economic Stagnation in India" in the *Economic Weekly* (special issue, June 1963) and another, "A Decade of Planned Development: The Indian Experience" in *Economia Internazionale* (May 1962).

Meanwhile, Governor Iyengar created a Research Division, whose members were to visit several central banks in developing countries. His idea was to encourage central bank cooperation in developing countries and to foster economic cooperation between India and these countries. I was selected to visit the central banks of Ceylon (Sri Lanka), Burma and Thailand and A.G. Chandavarkar to visit the African countries. The Governor wrote to the central bank governors of these countries about our visit. Once my programme was firmed up, I wrote to the central bank governors about the institutions I would like to visit. Rangachari, the Deputy Governor, objected that I was too junior an officer to write these letters.

Anyway, Dr. B.K. Madan smoothed things out and I went to these countries. Having talks with the central bank officers, government servants, business groups (including Indian businessmen), branches of Indian banks and the staff of the University of Rangoon, I realised that these countries had strong cultural links with India and hence India should establish trade and investment and other economic relations with them to mutual advantage. My report was discussed within the Reserve Bank. The Reserve Bank sent me to the Ministries of Finance and Commerce to discuss this report with L.K. Jha and K.B. Lall. All of them were appreciative of what I had recommended.

However, an amusing and embarrassing incident took place within the Reserve Bank. I had in my report on Burma mentioned about the growth of China's influence in that country and suggested that India should exert itself to establish good economic relations with Burma before it could come into Chinese influence. Rangachari objected to my discussing political issues; he thought that I had ventured into themes for which I was not competent and authorised by the Reserve Bank to dwell on these issues. Dr. Madan intervened and convinced Rangachari that I had done this in good faith. Still this part of my report was modified before it was sent to the government.

In this connection, I should mention my encounter with Morarji Desai, who was then Finance Minister. He was a friend of my grandfather and father. Having known about my report, he invited me to meet him to talk about my visits. When I met him, he was spinning on his charkha, yet he listened very patiently to what I said about the importance for India to cultivate good economic relations with these countries. At the end of it he said, These are small countries which do not matter for us so much as the United Kingdom and the United States. I argued with him but to no effect. I feel in retrospect that our failure to establish good, fruitful economic relations with these countries, which in fact experienced a growth rate much greater than ours, has been to our disadvantage. Such was our foreign economic policy at that time of neglecting the countries of South East Asia.

At the end of 1963, the UK government invited four Indian economists to visit the UK so as to improve relations between India and the UK. I was selected by the Reserve Bank along with Dr. Ghosh from the Planning Commission, Dharm Narain from the Institute of Economic Growth and Pai Panandiker from the Indian Chamber of Commerce. We were treated as Her Majesty's guests and were put in touch with officers of the government, Bank of England and Chambers of Commerce. We discussed with them the Indian experience of planned development during a decade of our experience. We also met Harrod and Balogh at Oxford University. Harrod wanted to visit India to understand Indian economic policies. Pai Panandikar promised to invite him to India on behalf of the Indian Chamber of Commerce, which he later on did. Balogh met Ashok Mehta, Deputy Chairman of the Planning Commission, just a few days prior to our visit. We asked him about his discussions with him. He said, "He is an ass." On further questioning, he repeated,

"He is a stupid ass." Maybe he found him rather woolly and incompetent to guide the Planning Commission.

Later on, we visited Cambridge University to meet Joan Robinson, Nicholas Kaldor and Richard Goodwin—all of whom we had met in India in 1956-1958. At our request, A.K. Dasgupta was also invited to meet us. It was a great pleasure to renew my acquaintance with all of them. Robinson took me to Kaldor's house to meet his family as also to Goodwin's house. She had strong likes and dislikes, but she was very friendly with me from the Poona seminar days. Later on I corresponded with her on some of my writings; she was very prompt in replying. I had sent her my papers on income distribution in India as well as on flow of funds.

At this time I wrote two articles on the controversy regarding balanced and unbalanced growth. I argued that the two approaches were complementary and criticised proponents of both schools for their one-sided approach. These articles were the result of my thinking about Indian planning for economic development. Later on one article, "Theories of Balanced and Unbalanced Growth: A Critical Appraisal", was published in *Kyklos: International Review for Social Sciences* (vol. XVII, 1964) and the other, "Some Notes on Balanced and Unbalanced Growth", in the *Economic Journal* (March 1965).

By this time I was invited to join the United Nations Asian Institute of Development and Planning as a Development Economist in Bangkok. The Reserve Bank permitted me to join this institute for two years—1964-1966. My experience at this institute will be presented in a later chapter.

During this time, Albert Hirschman, a well-known economic historian interested in economic development policies in developing countries by advocating a strategy of unbalanced growth, visited India and the Reserve Bank and made it a point to meet me to tell me how much he appreciated my article on income distribution in the *American Economic Review.*

I returned from this institute in early 1966. This was the time when the World Bank Mission (Bell Mission) was examining Indian problems. One of their proposals was to devalue the rupee. Instead of discussing confidentially with the Ministry of Finance and the Reserve Bank they, rather arrogantly, put up this issue for public discussion. I was not in favour of straightforward devaluation and suggested to the Economic Adviser Pendarkar to try out a dual exchange rate, as suggested by Nicholas Kaldor for developing countries. By this time, Pendarkar learnt that the Reserve Bank and the Ministry of Finance had already taken the decision to devalue the rupee. Governor Bhattacharji was in favour of devaluation without reference to the Bell Mission. And he carried the day. So Pendarkar did not submit my paper to the Governor, for devaluation was a *fait accompli.*

Later, the Planning Commission came out with the first draft of the Fourth Five Year Plan and sent it to the Reserve Bank Governor for his comments. Pendarkar asked me to review this document critically. I did this by pointing out that the draft plan had overestimated the availability of domestic and exchange resources, had suggested unrealistic output targets and seriously underestimated the demand for power. Pendarkar sent this paper with his favourable comments to the Governor, who sent it immediately to the Planning Commission. The Planning Commission members and in particular Dr. V.K.R.V. Rao exhorted the economic division to examine carefully its methodology for the estimates it made, in the light of my paper.

The Planning Commission referred my paper to T.N. Srinivasan (then consultant to the Planning Commission) and asked him to defend the method of estimation of power requirements. He wrote an article on this theme in the *Economic and Political Weekly*. Pendarkar and I thought that his method was completely unreliable and requested Venkatachalam of the Department of Statistics to point out its drawbacks. He wrote his article in the *Weekly* as a rejoinder to T.N.'s article, convincingly defending our method and pointing out the unreliability of the methods suggested by T.N. The Planning Commission then revised its estimates.

Bhattacharji was succeeded by L.K. Jha, a veteran ICS and a graduate of the Cambridge University and with definite views on Indian economic policies. He regarded education as a significant determinant of the vigorous functioning of a democracy as well as of the pace of technical change and development. He asked me to prepare a draft of his public lecture on Education and Economic

Development. In this paper, I emphasised the significance of education as pointed out by great Indian leaders like Gopalkrishna Gokhale, Mahatma Gandhi, Rabindranath Tagore and J. Krishnamurthy. He based his lecture on my paper. Later on, I enlarged this paper extensively and published a booklet on *Education and Economic Development* (published by the Commerce Research Bureau in English as well as Gujarati, 1970 and 1972).

Jha had a brilliant idea to estimate the development potential India generated during 1951-1967. He thought this was a good measure of Indian policies rather than the growth rate of national income. Divatia of the Statistics Department and I worked on this theme and devised the pace of growth potential on the basis of several indicators—more than a hundred—on the basis of factor analysis, worked out by Divatia. This was published in the *Reserve Bank Bulletin,* "On Measuring the Pace of Development", in April 1968. This was also published in *Banca Natzaionale Del Lavoro* (June 1969).

After three years of Plan holiday, the Planning Commission started working on the Fourth Five Year Plan. The government appointed a Resources Working Group, chaired by I.G. Patel (Secretary in the Ministry of Finance) with Professor Anjaria, Deputy Governor of the Reserve Bank, and me as members along with several others. In the Reserve Bank, we worked on Financial Planning and prepared a report, which was discussed by the group members. Professor Anjaria and I went to Delhi to submit this report to I.G. Patel.

Later on, the International Conference on National Income invited the Reserve Bank to submit papers on Financial Planning for its conference in Israel. I prepared one paper, "Savings and Flow of Funds: A Tool for Financial Planning." Divatia prepared one on Financial Planning. These were published in the *Reserve Bank Bulletin* (September 1969). My paper was also selected by the Conference for publication in the *International Journal of Income and Wealth* (1970). This was the first time that flow-of-fund analysis was used for financial planning.

By 1969, prominent commercial banks were nationalised by Prime Minister Indira Gandhi, purely for political reasons. L.K. Jha was not in favour of this policy. Neither was I. I wrote an article in the

Economic and Political Weekly (October 1970) criticising the move. Since it was a *fait accompli,* I suggested the manner in which the banking system could be used as an instrument for district development. I suggested that these banks should have operational autonomy, should be allowed to function in the light of their history and character in the light of objectives decided by the Reserve Bank and there should be no government interference in their day-to-day functioning.

The other populist move from the point of view of economic development related to curbing what was called the concentration of economic power of large business houses. R.K. Hazari, who researched this theme, traced each firm to some business house or the other. Nationalised commercial banks were asked not to provide credit for their working capital requirements without reference to the Reserve Bank. I criticised this approach, arguing that these business houses showed enormous entrepreneurial talents in creating a diversified industrial structure and needed to be recognised for their contribution to economic and industrial development. With this theme I wrote an article, "Monopoly and Public Policy", in the *Economic and Political Weekly* (30 May, 1970). These articles, criticising government policies with regard to nationalisation of banks and discrimination against big business houses, were written under my name. It is a tribute to the Indian tradition of recognising the individual's right of free expression of well-argued and substantive dissent from government policies that the Reserve Bank did not object to my publishing these articles.

Around 1968, Vikram Sarabhai (Chairman of the Atomic Energy Commission) came to meet Governor Jha with regard to two projects relating to atomic power in Uttar Pradesh and Cutch in Gujarat. He wanted the Reserve Bank to appraise these project reports. Jha called me to meet Sarabhai and asked me to appraise these projects. By this time, I had developed sound criteria for project appraisal—internal rate of return and exchange rate of the project. This was with a view to improve project selection and planning, which were not given adequate attention in the planning process.

In the light of these criteria I requested S.A. Dave and R.H. Patil—both of the Research Department—to appraise one project each, which they did very competently. With some modification, they concluded that these projects appeared to be sound and viable. The Reserve Bank sent these appraisals to Sarabhai.

Around 1967, the Administrative Reforms Commission appointed a study team to suggest changes in financial administration. Dr. L.K. Lakdavala, who chaired the team, requested the Reserve Bank to permit Deena Khatkhate and me to become its members. We worked hard on this project and suggested that for improving planning and implementing projects at the Centre as well as in the states, the government should set up a National Development Bank. This bank would determine the share of the Centre and the states in the resources on the basis of the Plan. However, it would not transfer the resources without appraising the projects. Actual disbursement would depend on its rational objective project appraisal in the light of Plan priorities and objectives. The funds of the bank, thus, would not be rigidly earmarked for the Centre or any state. If either the Centre or any state were unable to present sound projects with the required assistance equal to its share, resulting surplus funds would be diverted for use in states that had formulated sound schemes. This innovation, we argued, would improve project planning and implementation—an aspect neglected by the Planning Commission. We argued that in the ultimate analysis the success of a Plan crucially depends on effective project planning. The report of the study team was published by the government in 1967. On the basis of this report, we published an article, "Centre-State Financial Relations in the Context of Planned Development" in the *Economic and Political Weekly* (21 February 1970) and later in *World Development* (June 1978).

In Ceylon (Sri Lanka) the International Economic Association under the chairmanship of Prof. E.A.G. Robinson organised a seminar for participants from South Asian countries. Professor Anjaria and I participated from India. I contributed a paper, "On Inflation and Its Control", based on Indian experience. The discussions at this seminar were published later by the International Economic Association.

After the nationalisation of major commercial banks in 1969, there was a question of appointing members of the Boards of Directors. Initially, a Reserve Bank official was appointed as an adviser to the management. I was appointed as adviser to the Bank of Baroda and Syndicate Bank. At the management meetings, I examined all credit proposals on their merit, irrespective of what the government wanted. Later on the boards were constituted and I was appointed Reserve Bank nominee director of the Syndicate Bank. I have a suspicion that the Banking Department did not like my independent stand at the management meetings and hence I was dropped as a Director of the Bank of Baroda. However, T.A. Pai, the earlier Chairman of the Syndicate Bank, wanted me to continue as its Director.

In both capacities I tried to convince the Board members to adopt policies that would promote district development. I also suggested several development schemes for encouraging individuals to open new deposit accounts, and suggested criteria for appraising credit proposals. For all these purposes, I recommended reorganisation of the management structure of the banks. I wrote for these purposes several action-oriented memoranda for discussion at the Board meetings. The Board members liked these papers and I had their support.

These papers I circulated to all the Chairmen of the other commercial banks and the Chairman of the State Bank of India. All these papers I published in various issues of the *Economic and Political Weekly*, seven of them in 1970. These were not academic papers. They were meant to induce positive action by the banks to promote agricultural and industrial development. Later on, I published these papers in my book *Structures of Financial Institutions* in 1972 for inducing discussion among interested individuals and institutions, before leaving my position as a Director of the Syndicate Bank.

Let me mention how the boards functioned till at least 1972. Each bank had a nominee Director from the government and one from the Reserve Bank. The government nominee Directors were instructed by the Secretary of the Banking Department, Bakshi, to take a certain stand on the agenda at board meetings. They were not allowed to function as Directors who could take a stand on the merit of the credit proposals. The instructions largely pertained to credit proposals of large business houses and Bakshi's attitude was to favour such houses as he liked. Then the Deputy Governor of the Reserve Bank, R.K. Hazari, and Bakshi agreed that before the Board meetings the government nominee and the Reserve Bank nominee should meet and agree to take a common stand at the Board meeting. Most of the other directors more or less agreed to what these nominee Directors recommended, as they wanted to be in the good books of the Department of Banking, which had powers to appoint these so-called independent directors from the private sector.

I did not accept any instructions from the Reserve Bank. In fact, the Deputy Governor knew that I would not accept any such instructions. I also refused to discuss the Board agenda with the government nominee, when he proposed to meet me. I took the stand that each Director should take a stand on proposals on their merit irrespective of the attitude of the government. I was the only Reserve Bank Director who refused to meet the government Director before the Board meetings. Later on I asked Hazari whether he had agreed to such meetings by the Reserve Bank Director and the government Director. He said that he did. I told him that I did not accept this condition and would take an independent stand at the discussion on the basis of what I considered right. I got away from this tangle but, as I said earlier, I was not appointed as a Director of the Bank of Baroda, a major commercial bank.

The Department of Banking functioned as chief executive of the banks, without any accountability, and the Chairmen of the banks were treated as subordinate officers. This led to corruption on a large scale. This attitude demoralised the chief executives of the banks and affected their job performance. The result was that by 1990 the banks had become bankrupt (See my article in the *Economic and Political Weekly*, 12 October, 1991).

T.T.K., when he was Finance Minister, was responsible for two bright ideas: the setting up of Industrial Development Bank of India (IDBI) and Unit Trust of India (UTI). At this time, he also suggested that it would be worthwhile to work on incomes policy; for this purpose, he appointed a working group, chaired by Dr. B.K. Madan, to work on the relevance and context of income policy. This group met several times for discussion; and after this, Madan asked Deena Khatkhate to prepare a draft report, which he did and it was discussed in the group meetings. By this time, I had returned from Bangkok to the Reserve Bank. So Madan asked for my comments on this report. For this purpose, I prepared a detailed paper on incomes policy in developing countries, which he liked. In the light of my analysis, I told him that the draft report was excellent and the working group should endorse it. At Madan's suggestion I published my paper, which related to developing countries in general, in the *Economic and Political Weekly* (special number, August 1967).

In this connection I may mention that during my years at the RBI, the government involved the Reserve Bank in various policy discussions and policies. For example, Governor Iyengar candidly discussed in personal discussions and letters to the Finance Minister, Morarji Desai, on the importance of responsible fiscal policy, without which monetary policy cannot be effective. Morarji agreed with him. But Iyengar said: when you are the Finance Minister, we are confident that you would pursue a responsible fiscal policy but when you are not there, what would happen? Hence, he said that there should be some constitutional provision for restricting the government from resorting to deficit financing. Further, as I have already mentioned, Dr Madan was a member of the Income Distribution Committee, and Professor Anjaria was chairman of the sub-group of the Resources Working Group, chaired by I.G. Patel. And it is not generally known that the devaluation of the rupee in 1966 was primarily at the instance of the Governor, Bhattacharji; he was the main architect of this policy, not the IMF.

But there are instances when the government did not respect the independence of the RBI and this was when the dynamic but erratic T.T.K. was the Finance Minister. When Governor Benegal Ram Rao argued that tax policy should not impinge on monetary policy by having a tax on financial transactions, this was the function of RBI, T.T.K. rudely and arrogantly criticised the Governor; the latter as a result resigned as Governor with great dignity and grace.

Of course, things changed after 1965-66, and the Reserve Bank became a Department of the government without any independence to pursue effectively monetary policy that it considered appropriate. Governor Jha was not even consulted when Mrs Gandhi decided to nationalise commercial banks. Things changed a little after 1991, when policy objectives of the government and RBI were similar. But formally, the Reserve Bank's independence is not recognised; the government has the final say on monetary and banking policies.

One function that the Reserve Bank performed till 1967 was to encourage critical discussion on national and international policies by providing space in its auditorium to a discussion group, led by Maurice Zinkin, A.D. Gorewala and R.S. Bhatt. Zinkin and Gorewala had retired from the Indian Civil Service (ICS) and were independent thinkers and believed in the open and free discussion of economic policies. In fact, Gorewala had started a journal, *Indian Opinion*, which was very critical of government policies. But the Reserve Bank still helped them by providing space for the discussion group's meetings. The group invited outside experts, academics, experienced civil servants and also visitors from abroad from academia, international institutions and the like. Once, the group invited Per Jacobssen, Managing Director of the IMF to discuss the policies of the IMF. At that time my Harvard professor, Alwin Hansen, was a visiting professor at the Bombay School of Economics and was invited to participate in the discussion. Jacobssen made, in some connection, a remark that Keynes was an ignoramus about the policies of international institutions like the IMF; he was merely interested in domestic policies. At that point Professor Hansen got up from his seat and with an authoritative voice said: "Mr Jacobssen, you do not realise that you would not be in a position as Managing Director of the IMF but for Keynes." Jacobssen, himself a good economist from Sweden, was nonplussed. For it is true that before anybody else, Keynes in his *Treatise* had recommended an International Clearing Union and was responsible for the establishment of the IMF, when he and his team participated in the Bretton Woods discussions, and agreement on the establishment of the IMF and the IBRD.

The Reserve Bank also provided assistance to foreign scholars by giving them office space and secretarial assistance. One such was Daniel Thorner, who had worked on Indian economic history and analysed how the Indian railways built by British businessmen led to private profit at the public expense. In the United States, under the McCarthy era he was considered as a communist and would have been persecuted for no reason. Hence, he came to India to work on Indian agriculture, while his wife Alice Thorner worked on women's problems. They carried out their studies with profound research. Daniel, in fact, travelled all over India to meet Indian farmers, by train, bus, bullock-carts and quite often on foot. Because of his firsthand experience, his book became a highly illuminating analysis of agricultural problems. This could not have been done even by historians, who rely on statistics and other objective data. Daniel and Alice became good friends with me as well as other economists and also with Sachin Chaudhuri, editor of the *Economic Weekly*.

The other American economist who came to the Reserve Bank was George Rosen to work on industrial finance in India. He wrote his book on this subject while he was at the Reserve Bank. It was a very competent review and analysis of industrial finance in India. I reviewed his book in the *Economic Weekly* with some critical comments on his discussion of the creation of bank money. While in India he married Kusum Parekh, sister of Savita Parekh, friend of Jayaprakash Narayan, the eminent socialist leader. They named their first son Siddharth, the name of the Buddha when he was a prince in Nepal. Later on, I met them in Bangkok in 1965-66, when he was the head of the US Aid administration in Thailand. We renewed our friendship and met quite often. On his retirement he became the Book Review Editor of *Economic Development and Cultural Change* and quite often requested me for reviews of books in which I was interested. I reviewed three books for him. The last time I met him was in Washington in 1990 or thereabouts, when he had divorced Kusum and remarried. I met both of them then.

Milton Friedman came to the Reserve Bank in the late 1960s and spent a number of days there. He was a great monetary economist who earned the Nobel Prize. It was a great education to discuss with him money supply analysis, on what we were working in the Reserve Bank and on the monetary impact on business cycles, which he had studied some years earlier. He had a great interest in meeting and discussing with all types of persons, not only economists but even laymen like taxi drivers. He was a very warm and affectionate person, without any ego or a superiority complex, though he was such a great economist.

On the basis of my experience in the Research Department during 1953–1972, I may mention what important and significant research work it did, which was appreciated by all the Governors and some Deputy Governors like Dr. B.K. Madan and Professor Anjaria and initially Executive Director J.V. Joshi, who was responsible for strengthening the Department.

Of course, some Deputy Governors like Sundareshan and some Directors of the operational departments considered research as a luxury and not relevant for the operations of the Reserve Bank. Sundareshan told a senior member of the Bank that the Research Department was merely an ornament and the Bank in fact provided employment to economists, which was not needed for the Reserve Bank's functioning. The operational departments' heads were even jealous of the research workers, for they had easy access to the Governor, who relied not only on senior officers at the Department but also on very junior-level Research Assistants. Governor Iyengar, in fact, knew which individual was doing the work he liked, irrespective of his or her rank. I have received his handwritten notes to ask so and so Research Assistant to do some work he needed. In fact, when he met us in the lift, he would ask what work we were doing for the Reserve Bank as well as on other academic subjects.

The Research Department during 1951–1972 was one of the most creative and effective departments, even amongst other central banks of developed or developing countries. It collected data, analysed them and published them in its Reports on Currency and Finance, Annual Reports and Reports on Trend and Progress in Banking. This was not an easy task as some important data had to be collected, through questionnaires (drafted meticulously) like the data on company finances, foreign assets and liabilities, some invisible items in balance of payments and sector-wise composition of deposits and loans of the commercial banks. The Reserve Bank has been involved with rural credit problems since 1939. To understand the problems of credit for various strata of farmers, the Reserve Bank took the initiative in conducting a rural credit survey—no other central bank had attempted it—under the guidance of Professor Gadgil. This helped in formulating policies with regard to rural credit. A two-volume report was published by the Reserve Bank. Such pioneering surveys and studies were not done by any other central bank during this period.

The department was also actively involved in improving the data base for planning. It did several studies for the purpose like estimates of saving and investment, patterns of income distribution, money supply analysis, non-inflationary level of deficit financing, development potential of the Indian economy by 1969, flow of funds as a tool for financial planning, impact of PL480 assistance on money supply, public debt and its relevance for open market operations of the Reserve Bank of India, and several other studies. All these studies were published in the Reserve Bank Bulletin.

At the same time, Reserve Bank economists did considerable research work on their own. These research papers (about 25) were published in international journals of repute (referred by peers) during 1953–1970. The papers published by the Reserve Bank economists were more than the papers by all other economists from the country combined—the economists at the Delhi School, Presidency College, Calcutta, Indian Institute of Growth, Bombay School and Gokhale Institute.

Of these papers, about 20 were prepared by A.G. Chandavarkar, Deena Khatkhate and me. Three or four papers were prepared by the Statistics Department researchers—V.V. Divatia, Kashi Sastry and Pani.

After 1970, hardly a few papers were published in such journals, in spite of the fact that the Reserve Bank recruited several highly qualified economists since 1969. One wonders why they did not have the motivation to do such research that could be published in international journals. Maybe by this time, the Reserve Bank itself became quite subservient to the government and even the heads of the Research Department—although able economists—did not inspire or encourage young economists to do significant research.

After 1970, a large number of papers were published by Indian economists settled abroad, either in the UK or the USA, in these journals. One may mention A.K. Sen, Jagdish Bhagwati, Padma Desai, Avinash Dixit, Pranab Bardhan, Meghnad Desai, T.N. Srinivasan, Vijay Joshi and several others. The economists in India with few exceptions did not do research that could be published in international journals. In fact, when Shills came to India in the 1970s to work on Indian intellectuals he visited us at the Reserve Bank. He wanted to know what research we were doing, even apart from our work at the Reserve Bank. He wanted to know the research papers we had published in international journals of repute (referred by peers); he did not consider any paper published in an ordinary journal which did not have referees.

4

Managing a Development Bank (1970–1972)

THE Industrial Development Bank of India (IDBI) was the creation of a highly imaginative dynamic Finance Minister—T.T. Krishnamachari. Explaining the rationale of this bank, he told the Lok Sabha: "Where a long-term view is necessary and a certain amount of risk has to be taken, the existing institutions tend, by reason of their statutory obligations and traditions, to be conservative, and cannot in any case be very helpful ... We are creating this new institution mainly for overcoming these limitations. We are envisaging the new Industrial Development Bank as a central coordinating agency, which ultimately will be concerned, directly or indirectly, with all problems or questions relating to the long- and medium-term financing of industry, and will be in a position, if necessary, to adopt and enforce a system of priorities in promoting future industrial growth ... the Industrial Development Bank, apart from discharging any or all these functions, as circumstances may require, will be in a position to undertake special investigations for proving the commercial feasibility of any important proposals and it will be able to help in providing technical assistance to various authorities or undertakings interested in industrial development ... It is in sum, a lender of the last resort, for all periods other than purely short-term periods, and for all or practically all purposes, as far as industrial enterprises are concerned. We have considered it desirable, in these circumstances, to provide for the ownership and management of the new institution being vested in the Reserve Bank of India. ... The Reserve Bank, I think, is today the institution which can most appropriately guide a development bank of this kind. The Reserve Bank is, and I hope it will continue to be, free from the pressure of political or other influences. It is in a position to take a purely objective view of our needs. I have no doubt that under the auspices and with the assistance of the Reserve Bank, the Development Bank will be able to discharge its fairly onerous burdens satisfactorily."

This was my conception of the role of this type of development bank. After I joined the IDBI, I tried in several ways to provide development orientation to this bank.

The first Vice-Chairman of the IDBI was Dr. B.K. Madan. He established several institutions or conventions, with the help of his able General Manager (S.L.N. Sinha), that enabled the IDBI to play its expected coordinating role. The first such institution was the monthly Inter-Institutional Meeting (IIM) for coordinating the activities of term-lending institutions like the Industrial Credit and Investment Corporation of India (ICICI), Industrial Finance Corporation (IFC), Life Insurance Corporation (LIC) and Unit Trust of India (UTI). It was at this meeting that broad policies in the field of project financing were discussed and coordinated and action taken with regard to the financial and technical assistance on a consortium basis for large as well as medium projects. After the project appraisal report was prepared, Dr. Madan established the convention of organising an Ad Hoc Committee of experts from the government as well as the private sector to discuss the appraisal report. The suggestions made at this meeting were taken into account for preparing the final appraisal report, which was discussed at the IIM, the share in financing by each institution determined, and then presented to the Boards of the institutions. Thus, all precautions were taken to consider the financial and technical aspects of the project. Thus a method was established to provide consortium finance to well-examined industrial projects.

Further, IDBI coordinated the activities of the State Finance Corporations (SFC) and the banks in the field of term financing through its assistance in the form of refinance of loans, bills rediscounting and refinance of export term credits as well as participation in such term credits.

Thus with Dr. Madan, IDBI did gain considerable experience and in spite of its young age did attain the status of a mature apex development bank.

Now I thought it was time to give development orientation to IDBI policies; so far it merely financed projects that were submitted to it for financial assistance.

In this context, the IDBI initiated exploration of the new promotional function that it could undertake. For this purpose, it was essential for the IDBI set-up to develop live and intimate contact with the economic situation and potentialities in different regions of the country. As a first step, the IDBI opened four regional offices and set up a regional committee with powers to sanction assistance up to a certain limit. This was with a view to shortening the time lag between project submission and assistance.

Then it started project work to assist private entrepreneurs on undertaking sound projects. Hence, it set up a Committee of Direction, comprising senior officials of the IDBI, the ICICI, the Agricultural Refinance Corporation (ARC), the IFC and the Industrial Financial Department and the Department of Statistics of the Reserve Bank of India to initiate surveys of industrial possibilities in relatively backward districts for the purpose of identifying concrete project ideas. These were discussed with the state governments concerned.

The next steps related to identification and search of entrepreneurs, preparation of detailed project reports and active implementation of such projects with the financial and technical assistance of financial institutions. The IDBI on its own could not undertake these functions. Hence, a new move was initiated to bring together state-level financial institutions, the prominent banks in the states, state government Industries Departments and term-lending institutions like IFC, ICICI, and ARC under the leadership of the IDBI to form an inter-institutional group.

The IDBI soon realised that it was not possible for entrepreneurs to prepare sound project reports, involving choice of technology and other technical details. There was a Kerala team of officials and economists that approached the IDBI and posed this problem. Thus, the idea of setting up a jointly sponsored and financed Technical Consultancy Services Centre (TCSC) for each state by the Inter-Institutional Group (IIG) evolved as a logical extension of the IIG work. This involved considerable discussions with the institutions concerned at seminars organised by the IDBI. The first such seminar was held in Kerala and after considerable discussions, the institutions agreed to sponsor a TCSC in Kerala. As a result, the Kerala Industrial and Technical Consultancy Organisation (KITCO) was set up. If this experiment succeeded, it was decided to set up such TCSC in each state. This was done during 1972-1975.

The State Bank of India did not participate in this venture. Here, I had a long correspondence with the chairman—Talwar—trying to obtain his support, but to no avail. Later on Talwar regretted his stand on this issue. He frankly told me later that he did not appreciate this approach at that time but he now realised that he made a mistake.

Such TCSCs with their limited expertise cannot undertake detailed project making, when the task required specialised expertise particularly for complex projects. Hence, to help TCSCs as well as private entrepreneurs, it became essential to encourage private consultancy services and acquaint them with the promotional task of the development bank. For this purpose, the IDBI with the assistance of other term-lending institutions prepared a list of available technical consultancy services in the country, on the basis of their experience with medium-large projects that they had financed. This list was circulated to all financial institutions, TCSCs, and even private entrepreneurs. They thus would know whom to consult for solving their technology problems. These consultancy services were induced to charge fees to institutions on a marginal cost basis.

To be effective project appraisal work has to be related to the work of project supervision and studies of completed projects assessed by development banks. For this purpose, the IDBI devised a new proforma for collecting and processing data relating to assisted projects and the research set up at the IDBI was strengthened for this purpose. These studies related to (a) assessment of the divergence between anticipated and achieved outcome of an assisted project; (b) analysis of inter-firm performance in the same industry group; (c) inter-industrial linkages with a view to identifying new projects; (d) technical and administrative gestation lags, and (e) projections for the next five years or so relating to investment, output, exports, imports and gross return to capital. The first such studies were published in the IDBI Annual Reports for 1971 and 1972.

So far no vital link was established, except in a modest way, between technical research and project work in the country. At the stage of technical appraisal of a project, the IDBI set-up has been trying to identify technological research problems that can emanate from the examination of a given project. The idea was to provide such problems to the technological research bodies—of which a list was under preparation—for their possible solution. A modest contribution to the field of linking technological research and industrial growth could become possible as a result of the IDBI efforts.

The IDBI was keen to promote projects based on indigenous research, if that proved feasible. As an example, it took the risk of financing a project—Swaraj Tractor—which was based on indigenous research at the Council of Scientific and Industrial Research (CSIR). No private entrepreneur was willing to take up this project and the central government was not inclined to support it but ultimately the entrepreneurs—scientific researchers who evolved this technology—got the support of the Punjab government. Then the problem of providing finance arose. No institution was willing to finance. The IDBI supported this venture, based on Indian research, after critically appraising the project. Such a step was in fact consistent with the IDBI functions as explained by T.T.K. in his speech in the Lok Sabha. (See my article "Decision-making in the Public Sector: Case Study of Swaraj Tractor", *Economic and Political Weekly*, May 1978, and also in the *World Bank Reprint Series*, 1978).

A development bank has to evaluate and appraise a project that requires its assistance. This is, indeed, a basic task that it has to perform, if the project has to contribute to viable and efficient industrial development. The IDBI and term-lending institutions were taking decisions on the basis of the financial viability of the project, its technical feasibility and sound management. However, it was found that these criteria were important but still might not result in the international competitiveness of the project. In that case, it would be desirable to import the product rather than produce it at home.

So the IDBI, after studying the extensive literature on this theme, decided in early 1971 on two criteria—internal rate of return and the implicit exchange rate of the project. The internal rate of return was to be consistent with development objectives—the suggested rate was 15 per cent per annum—and the implicit exchange rate—domestic cost of earning/saving, say one US dollar—was to ensure its international competitiveness. A suggested rate was to be lower than the official exchange rate. These criteria were adopted in a manner that these would not require data or accounting prices that could not be readily available to the Bank.

These appraisal criteria were discussed with all the project appraisal teams in several seminars with the participation of experts. Further, within the bank, V.S. Raghavan trained individuals who were responsible for project appraisal. The staff learnt how to apply these criteria very soon. In fact, there was tremendous enthusiasm for doing something different from what they were doing so far.

For the purpose of training, I prepared a paper indicating the manner in which these criteria were to be applied (See my article, jointly with Dr. S.A. Dave, "Criteria for Evaluation of Capital Projects" *Economic and Political Weekly*, August 1971). This paper was circulated to all the term-lending institutions as well as commercial banks.

Further, the decision lag—between submission of a project and financing decision—was shrunk and there were no avoidable delays. The Project Appraisal Department was strengthened and within the bank as well as at IIM, discussion was pointed and substantive. The IIM had the advantage of invaluable experience, with regard to industry and financing institutions, of H.T. Parekh (Chairman of the ICICI) and R.S. Bhatt (Chairman of UTI) with the guidance of V.V. Chari (Vice-Chairman of the IDBI). The IIM hence took quick and sound decisions about medium-large projects. In the IDBI, the responsibility of sanctioning financial assistance was that of the Executive Committee of the Board, comprising Jagannathan (Chairman of the IDBI and Governor of the Reserve Bank), V.V. Chari and Arvind Mafatlal and P.L. Tandon; the latter two had firsthand experience of industry and hence helped in taking quick and sound decisions. These two were active Directors on the Board.

Now that the IDBI business had grown and its profits were considerable, it was decided to resort to domestic borrowing on its own and thus reduce its dependence on the Reserve Bank. Further, to enlarge its resources, it introduced long-term deposit instruments and induced the projects that benefited from IDBI assistance to invest a part of their profits in these deposits. At the same time, it was decided to approach the World Bank for assistance; this was not primarily to obtain resources but to enable the IDBI to be aware of international thinking on industrial development. The World Bank mission, sent to appraise the IDBI project, recommended its approval to the World Bank. World Bank assistance was sanctioned in 1973, after I left the IDBI to join the World Bank's Economic Development Institute in September 1972.

I had, during my tenure at the IDBI, a completely free hand for taking the initiative in evolving the role and functions of the IDBI. This was possible because of the trust and confidence reposed in me by Jagannathan and V.V. Chari. Of course, I had the full and enthusiastic support of the staff, who experienced a kind of missionary zeal in strengthening the promotional role of the IDBI.

In particular I must mention the invaluable assistance I got from V.S. Raghavan, who because of his experience and very helpful nature and tact in educating as well as influencing the members of the staff created a sense of camaraderie and cohesion among his colleagues.

The other very valuable colleague was Sam Palia. He was highly intelligent, a person of great integrity and independent judgement and outspoken. He was a conscience-keeper of the staff.

Raghavan joined me at the Economic Development Institute of the World Bank. Later on he became a Director of a Department of the World Bank. Palia could have been a competent and imaginative Chairman of the IDBI but chose to do valuable public work among the tribals of North-East India.

Early in 1971, after I joined the IDBI, I was invited by ECAFE to participate in a seminar on Finance and Development for member countries. I was asked to chair this seminar because of my association with the Reserve Bank, IDBI and commercial banks. In this seminar I met Manmohan Singh, who represented the Ministry of Commerce for this seminar. Since then we have continued to be good friends. He is now the Prime Minister of India.

After the seminar, ECAFE asked me as a consultant to review critically India's performance during the first two decades. I did this later on and a part of my appraisal was published by ECAFE. I enlarged this paper and with the permission of ECAFE, published it as a book entitled *Two Decades of Development: The Indian Experience* in 1973.

During my tenure at the IDBI, there was no interference in our functioning by government officials. This was due to the ownership of the IDBI by the Reserve Bank. Thus, the hope expressed by

T.T.K. in the Lok Sabha that the Reserve Bank ownership of the IDBI would prevent any pressure of political or other influences and decisions would be taken on the basis of objective sound criteria was fulfilled.

All the initiatives taken by the IDBI were approved by the IDBI Board, in which the Secretary of the Banking Department of the Ministry of Finance (Bakshi) represented the Government of India. The Board appreciated the manner in which the Annual Reports presented in Chapter 2 the evolving role and functions of the IDBI (IDBI Reports: 1970-71 and 1971-72). The Board members also appreciated the manner in which reports were presented so much so that they considered the first chapter on Indian economic performance as much better than what was presented in the Annual Reports of the Reserve Bank. It may be mentioned that the Reserve Bank Board and the IDBI Board were the same.

After 1975, the government took over the ownership of the IDBI and since then government influence in the functioning of the IDBI became blatant as it did with the functioning of the nationalised commercial banks. The influence of politicians and government officials increased and as a result the IDBI could not function as a real development bank. A vital institution's functioning was thus undermined by the policies of Prime Minister Indira Gandhi. And so many other public sector institutions lost their autonomous functioning. The spirit in which institutions functioned for the economic development of the country before 1973 was overtaken by opportunistic policies of power-hungry politicians and bureaucrats who sided with them.

I anticipated this result and wrote an article opposing the move towards government ownership of the IDBI (See the *World Bank Reprints Series,* 1973 and *Commerce Annual Number* 1973).

Before such developments took place, I left the IDBI to join the Economic Development Institute of the World Bank (September 1972).

I may mention that during my tenure at the IDBI, we rejected an automobile project prepared by Sanjay Gandhi, son of the Prime Minister. We did not consider it to be a sound project. Thus, there was no political interference in our work during my tenure at the IDBI.

5

At the Asian Institute of Economic Development (1964-65)

THE United Nations started the Asian Institute for Development and Planning in about 1963. The first Director of the Institute was Narayan Prasad, who earlier was at the Reserve Bank of India when I joined it. He requested the Reserve Bank to release me for two years to work as Development Economist at the Institute. The Reserve Bank agreed to his request and I joined the Institute in early 1964.

At the Institute, there was a very lively and highly qualified group of economists and social scientists. There were: R.M. Sundrum (who later on wrote an excellent book on Development Economics), Nasir Ahmed Khan from the Lucknow University, M.M. Mehta from the International Labour Organisation (ILO), Dr. Addie from the World Health Organisation (WHO), a French economist and Harbans Lal, formerly of the Ministry of Finance in India.

There were also a number of visiting teachers, including A.K. Sen, Sukhamoy Chakravarti, Tinberger, Sachin Chowdhuri (of the *Economic Weekly*), and K.S. Krishnaswami (of the Reserve Bank). Thus, the environment at the Institute was very agreeable for lively discussion on various aspects of development strategy, planning and policies. The one person who brought about a sense of camaraderie and cohesion among the staff was Sundrum, who with his wit and lively personality, arranged group meetings for coffee as well as for interesting discussions.

Then there were several friends working at ECAFE: Vinod Dubey (who later on joined the World Bank), T. Manoharan (who studied with me at the Bombay School), Kitamura (a highly respected economist from Japan) and some others. Thus there was a good deal of communication and discussions between ECAFE and the Institute. Then there were M.L. Ghosh (from the Reserve Bank) and Ajit Bhagat, whom I interviewed on behalf of the Reserve Bank and selected him as a Deputy Director of Research. Both were very helpful in our settling down in Bangkok.

The Government of Thailand had given accommodation for the Institute in the famous Chulalongkorn University campus, a beautiful campus built by King Chulalongkorn to encourage Thai students to equip themselves with modern education. It may be mentioned that Thailand (or Siam) was the only country in Asia which was not colonised by the western powers because of the tact and foresight of its kings. It accepted at first Buddhism from India and later adopted several Hindu customs and practices. It has beautiful Buddhist temples, where the stories of the *Ramayana* are also depicted in beautiful paintings. From the 17th century, its kings were called Rama—(the hero of the *Ramayana*) and the capital was called Ayodhya (which was the place where Rama ruled). The people of Thailand are very friendly and tolerant. Even if there is a car accident, there is no rancour. Both parties meet, shake hands and say *ma pan lah* (Let us forget who caused the accident). Society is very egalitarian and even persons from an aristocratic family would marry a commoner from an agricultural family. The king is the head of the country but behaves as a constitutional monarch. The royal family is highly respected and revered and it is the strong bond which keeps the country united and peaceful, in spite of several revolutionary but peaceful changes.

The Institute organised a three-month course on national economic management for senior government officials from all Asian countries. This was a course given annually in Bangkok. As a Development Economist, I had to conduct seminars relating to economic development. I organised my seminars under four headings: (1) "theories" of economic development (from the German Stage theorists to Kaldor-Hicks); (2) critical variables for initiating a process of economic development; (3) planning process; and (4) international aspects of economic development. I prepared several papers as a basis for discussion at the seminars and were such as to form a basis for a course on economic development and planning at the universities in developing as well as developed countries. Later on, these papers were published in book form, entitled *Some Aspects of Development Strategy and Policies* (Bombay, 1978). I used this as a text when I was an adjunct professor at the American University (in Washington DC), teaching economic development.

The Institute also organised courses for senior government officials in member countries, at the request of their governments. So I participated in such courses in Taiwan (Taipei), Indonesia (Bandung) and Iran. The most active participants were in Taiwan. In Indonesia, the black market rate for the US dollar was seven times the official rate. The United Nations officials there advised us to convert dollars into Indonesian *ruppias* at the non-official rate. This was a common practice among all foreigners as well as UN officials. It was possible to obtain Indonesian paintings as well as boutiques at a very cheap price because of this. In Indonesia, Khan and I availed of the opportunity to visit by car Jogjakarta to see the famous Buddhist monument of Boro Budur. Similarly, in Iran, we could visit the old capital of Cyrus and Darius at Persepolis, which had 2500-year-old exquisite monuments. Because of the long association of people who came to India (Aryans) from Iran and the strong link between old Persian and Sanskrit, we were able to convert the Greek names into Sanskrit—Persepolis as Parspuri; Cyrus as Kuru and Darius as Dara. The elite class in Iran at that time were quite westernised and the professionals had education abroad, mostly in the United States. The Industrial Development Bank of Iran was working very efficiently with the help of the World Bank. The latter considered this bank as one of the most efficient banks supported by the World Bank. Tehran at that time was a very prosperous city because of the rapid pace of urban development. However, the rural areas did not experience much development. Besides, the Shah's family accumulated enormous wealth by appropriating a large share of oil revenues. The backlash came with Muslim clergies rousing the masses against the Shah and his policies of modernising Iran. Such a fanatical religious movement led later on to the fall of the Shah's regime and made Iran a theocratic state. But all this happened much after we left Iran.

At that time, there was talk about the development of the four countries—Thailand, Vietnam, Laos and Cambodia—based on harnessing the great Mekong river for power, irrigation, flood control, etc. The example of the Tennessee Valley Authority in the USA was mentioned. However, no work so far had been done on this project.

So Khan and I decided to work on this project. To suggest the allocation of benefits and financial costs among the four countries we had to work on the basis of very scarce data and had to devise ingenious methods of estimating costs and benefits. The result was our monograph, *A Framework for Planned Economic Development of Lower Mekong Countries*. This was published by the Institute and ECAFE in 1966. After this, we did not expect much support for this idea within the Institute or ECAFE. By this time, I left the Institute to rejoin the Reserve Bank of India.

However, much to my surprise, this document was widely circulated among the staff of the Institute, ECAFE and the countries concerned and aroused a great deal of interest and excitement among them. As a result, ECAFE organised a seminar with the assistance of the Institute in Bangkok to discuss this framework in early 1967. I was invited by the Institute to take part in these discussions to explain our methodology of deriving the costs and benefits and their allocation among the countries concerned. The seminar approved our proposals and urged ECAFE and the Institute to take follow-up action. Much as ECAFE desired to take this initiative, its effort was frustrated because of the political turmoil in these countries.

The United Nations organised an international seminar on the theme of planning for development in Ankara, Turkey, in 1965. I represented the Institute at this seminar and presented a paper on "International Aspects of Economic Development." In this paper I suggested the time perspective for external aid to developing countries before they reached what Rostow called the takeoff stage. I also indicated the role of the IMF in creating credit for stabilising the prices of primary commodities, a suggestion made earlier by Keynes and Kaldor in a different context. This was published in the United Nations publication *Planning the External Sector* (1967).

In this seminar, India was represented by V.K. Ramaswami, whom I was meeting after a long time. He presented with great clarity the planning process in India. I found most interesting Michael Bruno's paper on "The Optimal Selection of Export Promoting and Import Substituting Projects." This gave the criteria for project selection for generating an efficient process of development. This paper used accounting or shadow prices for inputs and the derivation of these prices was a complicated process. Later on, on the basis of Bruno's paper, I derived the criterion of exchange rate of a project, that represented the domestic resource cost for earning or saving a unit of foreign currency (say a US dollar). This exchange rate so derived should be equal to or less than the official exchange rate. I applied this criterion for projects when later on I joined the IDBI, as mentioned earlier. Bruno's paper was published in the United Nations publication mentioned earlier.

Thus, I spent two years at the Institute. This was a rewarding experience. I had time to catch up on my reading and learnt about the conditions of other developing countries from my interaction with the participants who were very intelligent and vigorously participated in discussions at the seminars at the Institute. The Institute wanted me to continue at least for a year more. However, I was eager to go back to the Reserve Bank; also, the latter declined the Institute's request. So I rejoined the Reserve Bank in early 1966, which was quite a turbulent year for the Indian economy.

The Asian institute was patterned after the Economic Development Institute of the World Bank to provide training for senior officials of Asian countries. It was helped initially by the World Bank, which deputed its economist, Nayan Prasad (formerly of the Reserve Bank of India) to become its first director. In the initial few years, it established a good reputation for training and several countries invited the institute to hold training programmes—like Taiwan, Indonesia and Iran. At the time the institute had very able competent economists on its staff as well as very well-known economists as visiting teachers; all these I have mentioned earlier.

After I left, the institute gradually declined in importance. It did not attract good economists and did not cooperate with ECAFE to involve them in its training programmes. Further, Prasad had a feudal temperament and recruited staff which would toe his line; some of them were from India, whom he knew from his early days and the Reserve Bank. In addition, he did not have a vision of what shape the institute should take and hence the institute lost its early reputation.

The EDI had the support of the World Bank and its economists. Further, being in Washington, it could attract well-known economists to participate in its programmes. Further, since 1953, the World Bank appointed very able economists to head it. No such help was available to the Asian Institute, partly because of the feudal temperament of the

Director and his lack of vision about what the functions of the institute should be. Therefore, even Thailand was unwilling to support this institute; Singapore tried to help it by providing facilities. But to no avail; an institute even like the EDI of the World Bank (1970) almost disappeared from the scene after 1969.

By the end of 1970, I was to take up an assignment with the Economic Development Institute of the World Bank. However, Governor Jagannathan wanted me to become General Manager of the Industrial Development Bank of India. He did not even call me for a meeting but intimated by telephone that I should accept this position without arguing about the terms and conditions attached to this offer. I agreed on condition that after about two years, I should be permitted to join the World Bank. He wrote to the World Bank that he would release me for work at the World Bank only after two years. And so by the end of 1970, I assumed charge of the IDBI as General Manager. The Governor had consulted R.K. Hazari, who had strongly recommended me for this post as he had read all the papers I had submitted to the Boards of Directors of the banks earlier.

6

At the World Bank (1973–1990)

I joined the Economic Development Institute (EDI) in September 1972. This Institute was started by World Bank (President Eugene Black) to train government officials from developing countries. Its objective was to provide them with essential elements of development economics so that they could understand the complexities of the development process. The first course was on economic development for a period of about six months. This initiative by the World Bank provided enough time for the participants to absorb the teaching and at the same time establish intimate relationships among their colleagues from other countries, thus providing a communication channel for interacting with other countries. These participants established the Association of EDI Fellows in several countries like South Korea. Later on they occupied key positions in their governments and thus established cordial relations with the staff of the World Bank.

This course on economic development was shortened to six weeks when I joined the EDI and was named as a course on National Economic Management. There were other six-week courses on Evaluation of Industrial Projects, Evaluation of Agricultural Projects and Evaluation of Education Projects.

When I joined I proposed a course on Development Banking. The World Bank supported industrial financial companies in several countries and their staff required some training for building their capacities for promoting industrial development. I thought, because of my experience at the IDBI, that these institutions could play a significant role in promoting a viable process of industrial development in these countries. Such was the rationale for my proposal for introducing this course on development banking.

My proposal was discussed within the EDI and was presented to the Industrial Finance Department of the World Bank for comments from its staff. The proposal was accepted by the EDI as well as the World Bank. Consequently I started to develop the contents of this course. As I wanted assistance from a person who had worked in a development bank in a responsible position, I suggested to the EDI to invite V.S. Raghavan of the IDBI to join the EDI. As mentioned earlier, Raghavan was critically associated with all the initiatives taken by the IDBI during my years at the IDBI. Before he rejoined the IDBI he had participated in the course on industrial project evaluation very actively and was judged by the EDI as the best participant of that year. EDI accepted my suggestion to invite Raghavan in 1973. We together worked out the details of the proposed course.

In the first year, Raghavan and I participated in the course on National Economic Management in Nigeria. This course was conducted by the EDI jointly with two professors of the Nigerian University at the request of the Nigerian government. Both professors were very well qualified and their support was very valuable in conducting this course. The participants also were very active in discussions. We were amused to find that pan-chewing was not merely an Indian habit. Nigerians also had the habit. All the participants were chewing some type of narcotic leaves during the seminars. There were several hawkers selling these leaves.

Thus for two years, I participated in conducing several seminars in the course on National Economic Management and introduced for the first time the topic on Technology Policy, which enables a country to adapt creatively modern technology suited to its resource endowments. This made me write a paper "On Technology Policy and its Institutional Frame" (published in *World Development*, September 1975 and in *World Bank Reprint Series*). The other sessions I took were related to development strategy and policies, particularly in the sphere of financial aspects of development planning. For this purpose I prepared a paper "Economic Development: An Analytic-Historical Perspective" (later published in *World Development*, July 1976).

Then Raghavan and I conducted two International Seminars on Development Banking with the assistance of some World Bank staff and outside experts. For this purpose I prepared three papers based on my reading and experience of managing the IDBI—(1) Development Banking: Top Management Tasks and Structure; (2) On a Development Bank's Selection Criteria for Industrial Projects; and (3) Financial Institutions and Technology Policy. All three were published by the World Bank in *Aspects of Development Bank Management* (edited by William Dramond and V.S. Raghavan). Raghavan and I prepared two case studies for decision-making based on project appraisal of two industrial projects. For this purpose, participants were divided into two groups, one for accepting the project and the other for modifying or rejecting it. This led to spirited discussion among participants, based on what they had learnt from the seminar and their own experiences in the development banks they represented.

At the end of the second seminar, I proposed to the participants to work for an Asian Association of Development Banks. This was supported by William Diamond, who was responsible in the World Bank for promoting and supporting development finance institutions in developing countries, when he delivered the valedictory lecture at the end of the seminar. The lead was taken by the Chairman, A. Gasem Kherajdjou of the Industrial and Mining Development Bank of Iran. Consequently some such Association was formed. This has held annual meetings of the chairmen of member development banks for exchanging information and experience with regard to development bank functions and role in industrial development.

The Nigerian government requested the EDI to formulate a design for an EDI type of institution for the training of government officials on issues related to development strategy and policies. EDI formed a group of three persons—a senior official from Nigeria, a senior official from the Ministry of Finance in Brazil and me—to work out the details for such an institute. We spent a little more than a month in Nigeria, interviewing government officials from various parts of the country, university professors and other research institutions. We travelled to meet local officials and others interested in this project. At the end of our discussions we prepared a draft proposal for the institute. I discussed this report with my colleagues, Stevenston of the EDI (who was then in Nigeria) and Edward Lim, the resident representative of the World Bank in Nigeria. After their comments we discussed this draft with the government officials concerned. All of them approved the draft proposal and we sent the final version to the

Government of Nigeria in a few months after I returned to Washington.

My term at the EDI was to end by 1975 and I was eager to return to the IDBI. However, by this time Indira Gandhi declared emergency in India, which made it impossible to function in a responsible position without government interference. Meanwhile, the World Bank offered me a position as Chief of the Public Finance Division of the Economics Department. I hesitated for sometime but in view of the political atmosphere in India accepted the offer after getting permission from the Reserve Bank to continue in the World Bank for three more years.

As a Division Chief I promoted two research projects—one on Financial Structure and Policies for Development and the other on Management of Public Enterprises.

For research on the broad topic of Finance and Development, I indicated in my paper "Interest Rate, Transaction Costs and Financial Innovations" the major theme of this research. This theme was the role of financial innovations in evolution of the widening and deepening of credit markets. This paper indicates, by some case studies, the characteristics of the innovations that reduce the transaction costs for lenders and borrowers in developing countries, particularly for the financing of small enterprises and agriculture. This led to research on transaction costs, particularly for the small enterprise sector, in some developing countries.

These studies related to the Philippines (Transaction Costs of Credit to the Small-Scale Sector", by Katrina Saito and Dan P. Villanuva), Brazil ("The Commercial Banking Industry in Brazil, 1964-1974" by Sahid Yusuf) and Mexico ("Non-Interest Costs of Lending and Borrowing" by T. Riley). The other research studies related to informal credit markets; one on India ("Informal Credit Markets" by T.A. Timberg and C.V. Aiyer) and the other on South Korea ("The Unorganised Financial Sector in Korea, 1945-78" by Yung Chul Park). These studies showed how agriculture and small enterprises sector faced a financial constraint because of high transaction costs in these markets.

These studies indicated the urgency of cost-risk reducing financial innovations for lenders and borrowers. So several studies were made on the nature of such innovations in some countries. Some case studies were undertaken for this purpose. These related to "Innovations in Banking, the Indian Experience" by C. Rangarajan; "Innovations in Banking, the Gujarat Experiments" by V.G. Patel; and "Innovations in Banking: The Syndicate Experience" by N.K. Thinglaya. One such study related to the role of technical consultancy services in reducing risk by proper choice of technology to both the lenders and borrowers in small industrial enterprises. The Industrial Development Bank along with other financial institutions promoted such services in various Indian states. This experience was critically examined in a study on "Financial Institutions and Technical Consultancy Services" by Dr. B.K. Madan, Director of the Management Development Institute, Delhi. This study showed how these services were helpful in the choice of technology by the small enterprises, thus reducing risk to both lenders and borrowers. This promotional function of the financial institutions later on did not receive adequate attention in policies after 1975.

There are several other studies like determinants of saving behaviour. There was one on the significance of financial institutions for economic development; this was a draft for a lecture by the Presidents of the World Bank. This was liked by Macnamara, but he wanted to discuss other aspects of development. Then there was a critical review of the banking system in Sri Lanka by Jamshed Gandhi. There was a study on the impact of coexistence of organised and unorganised markets on the design of projects in the private sector (Allen Roe).

All these studies were brought out in the domestic finance studies (World Bank, Economic Department).

Because of the research done in the Division under my guidance, the World Bank requested me to lead two missions—in Kenya and in Tanzania—to study the financial systems in these countries and recommend measures to strengthen these systems. The report on Kenya was prepared by Gobind Nankani, Saito and me and was discussed in a seminar organised by the Central Bank while we were still in Kenya. The study on Tanzania was prepared by Gobind Nankani and me. This was discussed with the officials and the Governor of the Central Bank while we were in Tanzania. These studies were brought out by the World Bank for limited circulation.

Our Public Enterprise Project was opposed by Chenery (Vice President, World Bank) but had strong support from the President, Robert Macnamara, and Executive Director from India. The Director of the Economics Department, Abramovich, was also keen to institute this research. Chenery did not like my part in initiating this research but he could not oppose something that was supported by the Executive Director of the Bank. His relations with me after this were not as cordial as I would have liked. He had a vindictive streak in his make-up as several others also noticed—including I.G. Patel. Anyway, this project was initiated and some research studies were prepared.

One was on the Management of Turnaround in Public Enterprise Performance in India (by Pradip Kandwala). This indicated the policy measures required for improving public enterprise performance. The other was on Public Enterprise in Italy by Prodi. I made a case study of a successful public enterprise—the Swaraj Tractor project in India—which I supported when I was in charge of the IDBI—which indicated the importance of public sector-private sector collaboration for managing a public enterprise. In this case, government ownership was less than 50 per cent and the manager-entrepreneur was from the private sector. Thus the government intervention was minimal and the management had full autonomy of functioning. This was also a project where the IDBI played a major role in financing a project with untried technology. I supported the project when I was in charge of the IDBI. This was the Swaraj Tractor Project; I prepared a paper on this project, based on my personal involvement.

These studies were also brought out initially in the Domestic Finance Studies of the World Bank. My detailed study on the basis of my personal involvement was published later in the *Economic and Political Weekly* (May 1978). An abridged version was presented by me at a seminar organised by Harvard University and was published in Leroy P. Jones (edited), *Public Enterprises in Less Developed Countries* (Harvard University Press, 1982).

The US Pugwash Committee sponsored a Symposium on Social Value and Technology Choice in an International Context and invited me to present a paper on India (Wisconsin, Wingspread, June 1978). I was thinking of technology choice since my Harvard days and emphasised the importance of a deliberate technology policy to adapt and improve creatively modern technology. I felt that the discussion on development strategy which took place before and after independence, though intelligent and imaginative, failed to emphasise the critical problems of technology policy. Hence I presented a paper at the Symposium on "Development Problem, Strategy and Technology Choice: Sarvodaya and Socialist Approaches in India." This was published in a book by Pugwash Committee later on. An abridged version of the paper was published in *Economic Development and Culture Change* (October 1982).

In 1980 I suffered from heart conditions and hence did not want to work as Division Chief, which required considerable administrative work. So I rejoined the EDI—an institute I always liked—in early 1981.

By this time the Association of Development Finance Companies (most of them supported by the World Bank) was already formed. This was the result of the idea I had mooted in 1975, as mentioned earlier. Hence, I thought about a Seminar of Chief Executives of Development Banks with a view to promote exchange of ideas and experiences with regard to the role of development banks in promoting industrial development. The first such seminar was organised by William Diamond (an architect of the World Bank policy towards supporting and promoting industrial finance companies) and V.S. Raghavan, who had earlier helped me in organising courses on Development Banking in 1974-75. So I thought it was time for a second Seminar for Chief Executives, entirely managed by them. Unlike the first seminar, this was meant to discuss papers prepared by Chief Executives, rather than arranging lectures by experts. These seminar discussions were practically managed by the Chief Executives, each one of whom chaired a session.

For this International Seminar I prepared several papers based on my experience as Chief Executive of the IDBI during 1969-1972. These were: (1) "Development Banks as Catalysts for Industrial and Financial Development" (published later in the *International Journal of Development Banking*, 1993); (ii) "Financial Institutions and Technical Consultancy Services (TCSCs): the Indian Experiment in Small Enterprise Promotion" (published as *EDI Seminar Paper 24* and later in the *Journal of Development Planning* (United Nations, New York, no. 18, 1988). The latter was a critical review of the performance of the TCSCs promoted by the IDBI at my initiative in 1972. I also circulated a paper on "The Industrial Development Bank of India: A Decade of Experience" (published in *Commerce Annual Number* 1975 and also as *World Bank Reprint Series*, no. 18).

This international seminar was very fruitful and provided an opportunity to the Chief Executives to exchange experiences and establish close relationships amongst themselves. India was represented by Dr. S.A. Dave (IDBI), Nadkarni (ICICI) and Talwar (ex-Chairman of the State Bank of India as also the IDBI).

At the end of the seminar I suggested that the banks should start an International Journal of Development Banking, as a forum for the discussion of issues relating to development banking. The participants liked this suggestion and Nadkarni announced his decision to start this journal by the ICICI. In 1984 he called a meeting in Bombay of all the financial institutions at the inaugural ceremony of the journal, mentioning that this suggestion was made by me at the international seminar. This meeting was presided over by Manmohan Singh, Governor of the Reserve Bank. This journal has been publishing valuable papers on development banking since then.

As I introduced the theme of development banking for EDI programmes, I now took the initiative for two additional programmes. One on Financial Institutions, Technology Policy and Project Planning or Evaluation and the other on Public Enterprise Management. At the same time I suggested to the EDI that seminars/courses should be held in developing countries, for two reasons: one was to induce developing countries to start EDI type of institutions; the other was to reduce financial costs to the EDI. The countries which agreed to start EDI type programmes were to provide resources for all the domestic costs of the programmes, while EDI was to bear the foreign exchange costs. The EDI under the director Willoughby accepted these suggestions.

Accordingly, I visited several countries to discuss these ideas. The Central Bank of the Philippines agreed to hold an international training course on Finance and Development in 1984. The IDBI agreed to hold programmes on Finance and Development as well as Public Enterprise Management. Since 1983 it held two programmes on Finance and Development and two on Public Enterprise Management. The ICICI agreed to hold a programme on Finance and Development in 1987. The Public Enterprise Institute at Lubliana (Yugoslavia) held one International Seminar on Public Enterprise Management in 1985. The Institute in Kenya held one programme on Public Enterprise Management in 1986.

The Government of China invited the EDI to hold several programmes on Finance and Development for its officials in Beijing. EDI agreed and held four such programmes during 1983-1988. My colleague Hyung-Ki Kim and I prepared reading material for these two programmes—"Readings in Public Enterprise Management" and "Readings in Finance, Technology Policy and Project Planning" during 1984 and 1985.

For the Finance and Development theme, I prepared two research papers—on "Financial Innovations and Credit Market Evolution" (published later in the *Economic and Political Weekly*, 30 May, 1987) and "On Participating in the International Capital Market" (later published in the *Economic and Political Weekly*, 1989).

For the Public Enterprise Management I prepared two papers—on "Institutional Framework and Public Enterprise Performance" (published later in *World Development*, 1984) and a case study of a successful public enterprise management which adopted a recently developed technology—"Decision Structure, Technology Choice and Public Enterprise Performance" (published later in the *Economic and Political Weekly*, August 1988). Both papers indicated that public enterprises can be successful if they have partnership relations with the private sector and function in a competitive environment.

In 1987 the IMF invited me to participate in the International Seminar on Beyond Adjustment in Bombay. At this seminar I submitted a paper—"Structural Adaptation and Public Enterprise Performance". This was later published in the IMF publication *Beyond Adjustment: The Asian Experiences* (edited by Paul Streeten, Washington DC, IMF, 1988).

In 1988 the United Nations organised a seminar on Public Enterprise Management in Bombay and invited me to present my paper—"On Competitive Impulses and Public Enterprise Performance" (published later by the United Nations as also in the *Economic and Political Weekly*, May 1989). In this paper, I suggested on the basis of international experiences that public enterprise performance has historically depended on its functioning in a competitive environment. In the absence of such an environment, particularly for non-traded goods, it is possible to generate competitive impulses in other ways.

While arranging the EDI collaboration with the IDBI, I had suggested to the IDBI that such collaboration should result in starting the IDBI an EDI type of institution for organising international seminars on various themes. My purpose was to generate contacts—non-official—between India and the less developed countries for creating an environment for international cooperation. Such personal contacts were essential for mutual understanding among developing countries.

The IDBI accepted this suggestion and requested the EDI to assist them in formulating the design of such an institute. As a result, I visited India and contacted several research and training institutes that could cooperate with the IDBI institute in its programmes. I submitted my report both to the EDI and the IDBI on the Objectives, Scope, Functions and Structure of a Development Finance and Management Institute.

The IDBI did start such an institute—called Jawahar Institute—in Hyderabad. As normally happens in India, the physical structure was developed but the *raison d'être* of the institute has been forgotten. It has become one of several institutes in India. My idea of an International Centre (of the EDI type) did not materialise because the IDBI management lacked the spirit of innovation that prevailed in its early years.

Even the EDI has ceased to function as an international centre, which earlier created an environment of trust and understanding among participants from developing countries and established close personal relationships amongst them, so essential for international cooperation.

During my stay at the World Bank, I formed friendships with many eminent economists, such as Paul Streston and Ian Little, who had come to the World Bank as advisors. I used to discuss various issues with them over lunch or dinner. At that time, Paul was editor of the journal *World Development*. He induced me to publish some of my papers in this journal; I published several papers, which he liked, in this journal.

Ian Little helped me in my work on the banking system. Later on he formulated a research project on small enterprises. I reviewed his proposal in the light of my own work. He liked my comments and suggestions and acknowledged them in his book, which came out later as well as in his book on economic development.

Several other economists with whom I came in contact were Jagdish Bhagwati and Padma Desai (whom I knew well earlier) Deepak Lal, Amartya Sen, Vijay Joshi, Irwin Friedman and Andrew Kamarik (Director of the EDI). Thus my stay at the World Bank was very fruitful and very stimulating because of my contacts and discussions with them. And of course, my friendship with them.

7

Independent Consultant (1990–2000)

AFTER retirement from the World Bank, I was invited to be a consultant to the World Bank for some years. As a part of the World Bank mission to Yemen, I visited South Yemen and later the northern part. I had detailed discussions with senior officials in these two countries about industrial development and financial structure and policies. After my return to Washington, both Yemens were united. So I took the initiative in compiling national income accounts and other data for the united Yemen. I had to do this as I had to suggest industrial development strategy and policies and for restructuring its financial system.

For about two months I made an intensive study of the economy of Yemen in Washington. Both studies were discussed with the World Bank as well as with senior officials of Yemen. The industrial development study was brought out by the World Bank as its official document.

Hyung-Ki Kim at this time was in charge of EDI studies. He had worked with me for several seminars I had organised earlier on Financial Structure and Policies and Public Enterprise Management. Now the EDI organised a seminar for African countries in Finance and Development. However, they did not have even a single case study for any African country. Kim asked the EDI to invite me to prepare a paper on the financial system in Ghana. I prepared this EDI seminar paper on the basis of whatever data was available within the IMF as well as the World Bank. This paper was discussed at the EDI seminar on African countries. It was published as an EDI Seminar Paper.

The EDI was organising a seminar on Project Evaluation of Public Sector Projects. They had several studies on project evaluation criteria but did not have any study on the institutional structure for economic evaluation of projects. So they asked me to prepare an EDI paper on this theme, on which there was not much discussion in the literature. I prepared two papers on this theme, which were the basis for EDI seminar discussions. They were published as EDI Seminar Papers initially and one of them, "Institutional Structure for Economic Evaluation of Projects in Developing Countries", was published in the *International Journal of Development Banking* (July 1994).

The EDI, under the guidance and initiative of Hyung-Ki Kim, has undertaken since 1992 several studies on Japanese experience with regard to economic development that might be relevant to developing and former socialist countries. The first such study related to various aspects of the Main Bank system in Japan, designed by Masahiko Aoki and Hugh Patrick. Kim invited me to participate in this project and take part in seminars on this theme, in which several experts in Japan as well as distinguished economists from various countries participated. I took an active part in these seminar discussions. The final seminar was held to discuss various papers prepared by members of the research team. I was asked by the organisers to prepare a research study on the Lead Bank Systems in India. Because of my personal involvement and experience in the operations of these systems, I was able to do this study, which no outsiders could have done. All the papers prepared for this project, including my paper on Lead Bank System in India, were published by the World Bank in the book *Japanese Finance and The Main Bank System* edited by Masahiko Aoki and Hugh Patrick (Oxford University Press, 1994). On the basis of my participation in the various seminars on this theme, I prepared a study on the relevance of the Japanese and Indian systems for developing countries and the former socialist countries. This paper, "Main Bank System in Japan and Lead Bank Systems in India" was published in the *International Journal of Development Banking* (July 1994).

The second study undertaken by the EDI was on the Japanese Civil Service and Economic Development. This book was edited by Hyung-Ki Kim, Michio Muramatsu, T.S. Pembel and Kozo Yumamura and published by the Oxford University Press in 1995. Based on this study, Hyung-Ki Kim and I prepared a paper on the Japanese Civil

Service System and its Relevance for Developing and Emerging Market Economies. This was later published in the *Economic and Political Weekly* (1999).

The third research project undertaken by the EDI related to the linkage between non-farm rural small enterprises and urban commerce and industry. The research project invited experts from Japan and other East Asian countries to prepare research papers on case studies on this theme. Because of Kim, I was actively associated with this project and participated in several seminars to discuss papers presented by experts from various countries. I prepared a paper "On the Relevance of East Asian Experience: A South Asian Perspective." All these papers were published by the World Bank Economic Development Institute in the book *Toward the Rural-Based Development of Commerce and Industry* edited by Yugiro Hayami (Washington, DC, World Bank, 1998).

In 1991, the Government of Sri Lanka appointed a Banking Commission, headed by Salgado, who earlier worked in the Central Bank of Sri Lanka as well as in the IMF. He asked me to review critically the institutional structure of the financial system in Sri Lanka and suggest changes necessary to improve the system. I spent a month in Colombo to studying the structure of the system and suggested several institutional reforms. This report was discussed in a seminar organised by the Commission. For political reasons, the report was shelved and so were its recommendations.

I had critically reviewed the performance of the Indian financial system—and in particular the banking system—before 1990, after which the reform of the financial system was initiated by the new government under the leadership of Finance Minister Manmohan Singh. This was published later in the *Economic and Political Weekly* (12 October 1990) under the title "On Improving the Effectiveness and Efficiency of the Financial System in India." This paper showed for the first time how the losses of the banking system had eroded completely its capital base. This article was circulated by the Finance Minister to members of the committee appointed by the government to suggest financial system reforms.

This paper attracted the attention of the Indian Council for Research on International Relations (ICRIER) and the Director requested me to write a monograph on the theme. I completed this monograph with the help of A. Hasib, my colleague earlier at the Reserve Bank, in late 1992. This was published by the ICRIER in 1994 and was reviewed in journals like the *Economic and Political Weekly* and the *International Journal of Development Banking*.

Just after 1994, the Japanese government requested the EDI to arrange for seminars for the new entrants to its Foreign Service on the problems of developing countries. The EDI requested me to hold these seminars. I conducted about ten seminars on this theme, which were also attended by various Japanese experts on the problems of developing countries.

After 1997, I decided not to take any assignment for health reasons, though I continued to write for the *Economic and Political Weekly*.

In 1997 Dr. I.G. Patel invited me to give a lecture on a theme of my choice for the annual conference of the Gujarat Economic Association. Since I was going to India in early 1998, when the conference was to be held in Navsari in Gujarat, I accepted the invitation. I selected the theme on which I was working for some time, "Perspectives on Development". My friend A.G. Chandrasekar had suggested to me earlier to discuss three or four insights or visions in Schumpeter's sense into the development process. My choice was (1) Increasing Returns to Scale (Adam Smith, Allyn Young and Kaldor); (2) Marx-Schumpeter's Emphasis on Innovations and Entrepreneurship; and (3) Economic Backwardness in Historical Perspective (Alexander Gerschenkron's insight into the differential characteristics of the development process in relatively backward countries, compared to England during the nineteenth century). This paper was later published in the *International Journal of Development Banking* (January 2000).

My career would have taken a different course if I had decided to return to India in 1977. This was the time when the Janata government had come to power, with Morarji Desai as Prime Minister and H.M. Patel as Finance Minister. Patel immediately thereafter visited the United States to persuade I.G. Patel to become Governor of the Reserve Bank and me to become Chairman of the IDBI. He met me in Washington and peremptorily asked me to join the IDBI immediately. He requested I.G. to persuade me to accept his offer. I hesitated because of health and family reasons. However, Patel agreed to wait for two years. Meanwhile, he appointed J.N. Saxena as interim Chairman for two years. By this time the political situation had deteriorated in India and I thought that I might not be able to function independently and effectively. Then I.G. said that if I decided to return thereafter, he would appoint me as Deputy Governor of the Reserve Bank. I agreed. However, in 1980, I suffered a heart attack. I.G. visited me in the hospital and to make sure that I would agree to his proposal. I thought that I had now no option. Later in 1981, I met I.G. in Bombay to convey my inability to keep my promise because of medical reasons. I.G. was gracious enough to understand my predicament.

Shill Malhotra, Secretary to the Ministry of Finance, called me on telephone in Washington and conveyed to me the Ministry's decision to appoint me as Deputy Governor and wanted me to accept this offer but I explained why I could not. So the dice was cast and I continued in my much less stressful job at the EDI, till I retired in 1989.

In my career of about five decades, I was fortunate to find work in which I was really interested. I was not interested in mere administrative or power position. When I joined the IDBI, I had a plan or programme for the promotional role of the IDBI with regard to industrial development, and only that interest induced me to work with the IDBI. Once this purpose was served, I left the IDBI for the World Bank.

Because of my association with several different institutions with different objectives and functions, the range of my research projects and studies was quite broad. That led me also to undertake several case studies to illustrate my thesis. These related to public enterprise management and an innovative bank with unorthodox agenda and functions. These case studies were carried out because of my experience and involvement in these projects. Without that, it would have been difficult to undertake such detailed studies on decision-making. These studies have been used at Harvard Business School and Management Institutes in India.

I may mention that the themes for research and studies were chosen at my initiative and I was fortunate to obtain wholehearted support from the management of these institutions. Thus my work was always interesting and to my liking.

8

Retrospect on Indian Planning

INDIA has been a pioneer among developing countries in seriously thinking about socioeconomic development. Much before independence, its leaders and intellectuals were concerned about poverty and unemployment in the country and its lack of significant industrial development. The first book probably on the Indian economy by the Grand Old Man of India, Dadabhai Naorjoji, was *Poverty and Un-British Rule in India*. Since then, the struggle for freedom was thought of not merely as political independence, but as an essential step towards an effort to eliminate poverty and improve living standards. There was a general consensus among intellectuals and political leaders (in fact they too were intellectuals) about the objective of elimination of poverty and unemployment through political independence and radical socioeconomic reform for creating preconditions for a self-reinforcing process of general development. There was also a consensus about generating a process of development through a democratic form of government, with freedom of speech, association and personal liberty.

All the leaders were highly educated in India or abroad and were influenced by the spirit of the British system of government and the general discussion taking place about various social-political-economic issues among British intellectuals. Unlike the un-British rule in India, this heritage was a result of India's contact with British culture and civilisation.

After Gandhiji came on the scene, he organised the Congress party on a democratic basis with elections taking place at all levels. This was in a sense training and experience about democratic form of government. At the same time, the British granted reforms and generated participation by the Indians, in their own interest, through elections at municipal, provincial and all-India levels for selecting members of functioning bodies. Thus a consensus about democratic form of government with adult franchise was formed quite early in the freedom movement.

India's democratic functioning since independence in spite of poverty and underdevelopment has been due to the this early training and experience. Quite a number of thinkers had believed that after independence India would break up. For no other backward country had succeeded in establishing a functioning democracy, particularly in the context of a multi-ethnic, multi-lingual, multi-religious environment. India has been still a functioning democracy in spite of all her problems. With whatever other policy errors the leadership have made, this has been its significant achievement, which the international community is only beginning to understand.

However, in spite of this consensus with regard to basic objectives, there were sharp differences among various political and intellectual leaders with regard to the role of the state and development strategy. There were three distinct approaches or viewpoints. One represented by the *Sarvodaya* approach of Mahatma Gandhi. The other of relying on enlightened capitalism, represented by some conservative leaders like Vallabhbhai Patel. The third was the socialist approach represented by Jawaharlal Nehru.

Gandhiji's approach was to concentrate on improvement of technology in agriculture and small enterprises, as they were crucial from the point of view of elimination of poverty and unemployment. Urban industrial development, according to him, was meant to support and reinforce the process of rural industrialisation. But all these efforts had to be carried out by individuals and cooperative groups. He did not favour any role of the state that would stifle and suppress individual initiative and enterprise. He believed in what Thoreau said about government: the best government is that which governs the least. He strongly believed that the state is a soulless machine—a concentrated form of violence—which would suppress and control individual liberty and enterprise. To quote: "I look upon an increase in the power of the state with the greatest fear because, although while apparently doing good by minimising exploitation, it does the greatest harm to mankind by destroying individuality, which lies at the root of all progress." He was against all controls. Even after independence, he pleaded against even the control of food prices and the government had to abolish these controls till he passed away.

Vallabhbhai Patel's approach in some respects was similar to Gandhiji's. He was in favour of concentrating on agriculture and small enterprises. But he favoured a process of vigorous and rapid industrialisation. According to him, as with Nehru, it was not possible to protect India's independence in a turbulent world. For this objective, he wanted to rely on private enterprise as he believed that only private enterprise could accomplish this task because of its entrepreneurial talents. He would, therefore, support actively the efforts of private enterprises as long as they represented enlightened capitalism that served social interests. For him, without the active participation of the private sector with the efforts of the state, India would not be able to realise rapid growth and development, that would ensure elimination of poverty and unemployment and progressively improve living standards as well as the capacity of the nation to defend itself and play an active part in preserving world peace and prosperity.

The third approach was the socialist approach of Jawaharlal Nehru. He had been influenced by Marx, Fabian socialism and the success of the Russian five year plans. He was in favour of concentrating on the development of heavy and basic industries—the so-called commanding heights of the economy. These were to be owned and operated by the public sector—irrespective of its capacity to take entrepreneurial and business decisions. Private enterprise was to be permitted in other sectors; but it had to obtain an industrial licence from the government. Thus, private enterprise was to be regulated and controlled by the state. The objectives of eliminating poverty and unemployment were to be attained as a result of rapid industrial development.

After independence, with Nehru as the prime minister, his socialist approach was adopted by the government. The Planning Commission was constituted immediately after to formulate five-year plans. Generally this approach of state-initiated planned development had the enthusiastic support of the Congress party, all the young educated intellectuals and the leadership of socialist groups. The Patel type of approach had no support as the intellectual climate was anti-capitalist and anti-business. Only one prominent leader and intellectual of the old group, C. Rajagopalachari, publicly opposed this approach. In his opinion, this would result in suppression of enterprising individuals, who require freedom to operate according to their talents. Civil servants would dominate in making decisions with regard to development projects. Such a 'licence-permit *raj*', he said, would kill the spirit of enterprise and innovation and result in stagnation and slow growth. Hence he started his Swatantra Party, which favoured private enterprise and less of government controls and regulations. In his view, the role of the government is to create a climate favourable for the emergence of entrepreneurs with vision, imagination and business talents.

Nehru's socialist approach was formalised in a planning model by Mahalanobis, a highly accomplished physicist-statistician and intellectual. This model became the centre of attention and it was discussed by a conference of eminent economists. All these economists generally approved of this approach, except B.R. Shenoy, who submitted his minute of dissent on the ground that such a plan would result in deficit financing and hence inflation and at the same time create a climate for initiating a control regime, which would hamper the functioning of individuals and groups with entrepreneurial and business talents.

The young economists got much more interested in this formal model and their discussion centred around such models. The implications of this model for government policies was not discussed. That it was bound to result in a control regime, which would hamper growth and development, was not obvious to most economists. In fact, even Mahalanobis or even the prime minister probably did not realise that such an approach would result in the suppression of creative talents of individuals and result in political-bureaucratic domination of the decision-making process, resulting in inefficiency and waste of scarce resources. Such, indeed, was the result. Even after more than five decades of planning, poverty and unemployment still remain serious problems and even the objective of universal primary education, to be attained in a decade after independence, is still to be realised.

However, during the first fifteen years of planning, there was considerable enthusiasm among politicians, bureaucracy, planners and the economists and intellectuals. In this period all students who went to study abroad preferred to return to participate in the development process. There was almost a missionary zeal for working for development in a democratic framework. The leaders were mature, intelligent and far-sighted and the top civil servants were persons of great competence and expertise. At the same time because of freedom, it was possible to engage in public discussions about development strategy and policies. All this was reflected in the comments and articles published in the *Economic Weekly* edited by Sachin Choudhri. New institutions were set up for training in technology (Indian Institutes of Technology, IITs) and management (Indian Institutes of Management) in collaboration with foreign institutions of repute. The scientific establishment was strengthened, though somehow that was not linked with technological problems of industry and agriculture. Several universities were created and also several institutes for research and development. So able and intelligent students had considerable opportunity to acquire new skills and knowledge. The first three plans represented innovative insights about development problems and strategy and induced considerable public discussion. The business class too was helped in financing their projects by the creation of several institutions—Industrial Finance Corporation (IFC), Industrial Credit and Investment Corporation (ICICI) and Industrial Development Bank of India (IDBI). Institutions for rural finance and development as well as for agricultural research were set up and agricultural research with the support of the Ford Foundation led to what is called the green revolution.

The control regime was imaginative and development-oriented. However, after the death of Nehru and Lal Bahadur Shastri, politics was governed not by principle but by power politics and corruption. In 1966, when Lal Bahadur Shastri became Prime Minister, there was a general consensus on abolishing the control regime. If he had lived, things would have been different. However, politics took a different hue. The objectives of control were forgotten and politicians and bureaucrats started enjoying their powers over the economy. Politicians did not permit very able civil servants to take independent decisions, demoralising the civil service system. Hence, both politicians and bureaucrats developed a mindset that was geared to multiplication of controls without any development orientation. Big business got their way by bribing both politicians and civil servants, while new private entrepreneurs had no opportunity to function effectively.

This mindset had pervasive impact on academic and scientific research establishments. The administrative set up became more powerful than scientists or researchers, with the result that even the heads of these institutions too developed this mindset. Instead of merit, administrative regulations and power relations became the criteria of decision-making. This process was strengthened as a result of politicians and civil servants being appointed on the governing boards of these institutions.

As a result, there was complete disillusionment about the planning process and state control. Even those who had returned to India after their education abroad for participating in the development process found the environment not conducive to creative research and freedom of functioning in an environment governed by controls and regulations.

For example, some of the very bright economists who had returned after studying abroad left India to work in well-known universities abroad, particularly in the UK and the USA. Even those who remained in India were eager to go abroad to work in academic institutions as well as international institutions like the World Bank, IMF, and United Nations. Thus, the motivation and interest in doing significant research in India in the field of economics and economic policy did not flower in Indian institutions. Of course, in a large country like India, with its intellectual tradition, there were very bright researchers who still remained in India and did creative work in economics and economic policy. They found a very creative outlet for publishing their research results and commentary on Indian policies in the *Economic Weekly* started by Sachin Choudhry with the objective of generating Light Without Heat. This became the *Economic and Political Weekly* after 1964 and it widened the scope of the weekly to publish well-researched articles on politics, sociology, anthropology, demography, in addition to economics. However, most of the themes related to Indian conditions and policies. Since university departments became weak, there was not much incentive to do Ph.D. research. Those who wanted to do research went abroad.

Thus, educational institutions and even IITs and IIMs are facing a shortage of qualified teachers. The system has to change to create an environment of relevant research by able individuals in India as well as to attract Indians settled abroad to return for staffing research institutes and university departments, with a view to strengthening their ability to do research and thus train candidates for Ph.D. to take up important problems in university departments and research institutes.

The deterioration in the standard of teaching and research has been discussed by Deena Khakhate in an article in the *Economic and Political Weekly* (22 January 2002). To quote: "But all these evaporated after the 1970s with the emergence of new universities, intrusion of politics in academia and domination of trade unionism in the ranks of university teachers. Whether one published in a good journal or not, promotions were assured. Teachers could go on up the promotion ladder with the efflux of time. This was also the time when the best amongst the economists emigrated to foreign universities, more to work in a challenging academic environment than for pecuniary rewards. Indian economists trained abroad also avoided coming back, first because of the inhospitable academic milieu and secondly because there were enticing openings for promising Indian economists in American, British and Australian universities. The late S. Chandrashekhar, the Physics Nobel laureate, once said when asked why he had left for Chicago instead of helping his countrymen, that 'a scientist has to prove himself or herself every minute and you cannot do it in India, where the scientific temper is lacking' ... the malaise has gone too deep in the system and in the present era of venal politics to hope for a change is to ask for the moon."

The control regime led to a severe crisis and the government declared emergency, suspending all democratic freedoms. India became a dictatorial state without any idealistic principles, which governed policymakers during 1951-1965. However, democratic traditions and principles had struck such deep roots, that virtually all political parties other than the Congress united in opposition to this move and started a sort of Satyagraha movement for restoring democracy. This was led by veteran politicians who had participated in the Indian independence movement against the British, like Morarji Desai and Jayaprakash Narain, who were immediately arrested. With considerable public opposition to the emergency, the government was compelled to restore democracy and declare a general election, after which the opposition parties led by the Janata party won a significant victory and formed the government in 1977.

Meanwhile there was considerable public discussion with regard to the negative effect of state controls. Several Indian economists and well-known Indian economists settled abroad urged fundamental economic reforms. The need for reforms was recognised by the new government and those who succeeded later on. However, because of a lack of political will, the effort was gradual and halting. Then, India experienced a severe unprecedented foreign exchange crisis as a result of the policy of permitting short-term capital inflow in the form of Indian businessmen resorting to credit from international banks. This was followed by general elections, after which the Congress party and its allies came to power, with Narasimha Rao as Prime Minister and a distinguished economist with experience of almost two decades in policymaking, Manmohan Singh, as Finance Minister. Very courageously they virtually scrapped all negative controls, which had hampered Indian economic development. Even the government which succeeded the Congress party, the BJP and its allies, continued these reforms. In the elections held in the new century the Congress party came to power and formed a government under the prime ministership of Manmohan Singh, who continued the process of economic liberalisation. However, the government faces serious problems with regard to infrastructure—transport, communication and the rest—as also other areas like privatisation of public enterprises, labour laws, and rural and agricultural development. These problems have to be tackled at a time when the government faces severe resource constraints.

Even with these problems, the Indian economy has experienced, since 1990, an annual growth rate of 8-9 per cent. The reforms have also generated a feeling that India has now become a world power.

In this environment, for the first time intellectuals and professionals from the middle class became vigorous entrepreneurs and started enterprises in the sector of information technology. These enterprises have become leaders in this sector and have been responsible for the significant export of expertise abroad. In fact, the international community now has recognised the potential for growth in the Indian economy. It may be noted that these new enterprises had no government support.

The enterprises were supported directly or indirectly by Indian IIT graduates who had settled abroad. In fact, some of them returned to India to participate in this enterprise. This was a significant result of the post-1991 economic reforms.

Similarly, several economists settled abroad in international institutions like the World Bank returned to India after 1980 to participate in the development process. These economists either joined the government or research institutes and were significant players in the reform process. In fact, the climate for reforms was generated by the studies of eminent economists abroad. Even when they worked in the UK or USA they did significant research into the problems of the Indian economy. Several of them suggested as advisers to the government the design of the reforms to be implemented. Some who returned to join the government and research institutes took a significant part in advising the Finance Minister, Manmohan Singh, with regard to the reform process.

Thus, what was described as a brain drain from India earlier, proved to be a significant asset, not only for formulating economic policies after 1990 but also for creating an awareness abroad about Indian economic problems. They were thus responsible for cultivating intellectual interests abroad in the policy dilemmas faced by the Indian government. This development has been possible because of the democratic government framework adopted and implemented by Indian leaders.

Now that India is on the move, all Indians settled abroad have the rare opportunity of participating in the development process either from abroad or by returning to India. Of course, in a democracy in a multi-lingual, multi-religious and multi-regional country like India, with several pulls and pressures, it is not possible to carry out significant reforms in a short time. However, once the direction is chosen, it would be possible for India to attain its objectives of elimination of poverty and unemployment and achieve rapid growth and development. It would result in making India a significant player in international affairs, for world peace and prosperity.

9

Profound Insights into the Development Process

Introduction

Development or socioeconomic change or evolution is a unique historical process, determined by subtle and complex interactions among economic, social, political and cultural factors. The nature of these interactions changes over time and depends on specific historical contexts and institutional conditions. Hence, it is not possible to formulate a general theory of development or socio-economic evolution.

However, we do have what Schumpeter calls "visions" or intuitions or insights about the process of economic evolution or change. In this paper, I want to deal with three or four major—and what I consider to be the most profound—insights about the development process. The first is that of the political economist Adam Smith, which was later elaborated by Marshall, Young and Kaldor. The second is due to two sociologists-economists, Marx and Schumpeter. And the third is that of an economic historian, Alexander Gerschenkron.

Other economists/historians would have different views; however, if even a few of them consider only three such insights or visions, which in their judgement are significant contributions to development literature, we may be able to arrive at some consensus about the strategic factors in the historical development process.

Increasing Returns and Economic Progress

Smith in his first three chapters of *Wealth of Nations*[1] suggested that manufacturing activities were subject to the "law of increasing returns" because of the circular cumulative interaction between the extent of the market and division of labour, which he illustrated by his famous example of pin-making. The greater the market, the greater the scope for differentiation and specialisation. To this, Marshall[2] introduced the idea of "induced inventions" as a distinct factor in the growth process. Allyn Young in his classic article on "Increasing Returns and Economic Progress"[3] regarded the Smith relationship between division of labour and extent of the market as "one of the most illuminating and fruitful generalisations which can be found anywhere in the whole literature of economics."

Elaborating on this relationship, Young emphasised that increasing returns is a "macro-phenomenon" precisely because so much of the economies of scale result from increased differentiation, new processes and new subsidiary industries, that cannot be "discerned adequately by observing the effects of variations in the size of an individual firm or of an individual industry." Economies of scale are derived not only from the expansion of any single industry but from a general industrial expansion, which should be seen, as Young put it, "as an interrelated whole."

Basing his theory on Young's contribution, Kaldor[4] emphasised that

> ... the dominant influence on the rate of economic growth seems to be the growth rate of manufacturing output (together with ancillary activities, public utilities, and construction). This is so not only because the growth rate of productivity in the industrial sector itself rises but also because the growth rate will tend to increase the rate of productivity growth in other sectors. This may happen both in agriculture and in the distribution trades, partly on account of the absorption of surplus labor and partly because of a factor increase in the flow of goods into consumption. But, more generally,

1. Smith, Adam (1970). *The Wealth of Nations*, Andrew Skinner (ed.). London: Penguin Books.
2. For Marshall's contribution, see Schumpeter Joseph (1951). "Theoretical Problems of Economic Growth" in Richard V. Clemence (ed.) *Essays of J.A. Schumpeter*. Cambridge, Mass.: Addison-Wesley Press.
3. Young, Allyn (1928). "Increasing Returns and Economic Progress", *The Economic Journal* 38(152), December.
4. Kaldor, Nicholas (1967). *Strategic Factors in Economic Development*. New York: Cornell University Press. pp.23 and 54.

> industrialisation tends to accelerate the rate of change of technology, not just in one sector, but in the economy as a whole...there can be little doubt that the kind of economic growth, which involves the use of modern technology and which eventuates in high real income per capita, is inconceivable without industrialisation. In that sense there are no alternative roads to economic development.

The development process may, however, slow down or may be interrupted by supply constraints particularly in the form of balance of payments constraints. Hence

> it is impossible for a country ... to pass through successive phases of economic development, except when it succeeds in raising its export potential *pari passu* with the growth of domestic output. Bismarck's famous statement 'We must export or die' showed that he thoroughly understood the theories of Friedrich List.[5]

It may be noted that Hicks[6] based his theory of the rise and expansion of the exchange or mercantile economy principally on the insight of Adam Smith.

Process of Creative Destruction

For Schumpeter too, adaptive response is important; however, according to him, what is significant about the actual historic evolutionary process under capitalism is the introduction of innovations: new consumers' goods, new methods of production or transportation, discovery of new markets and new forms of industrial organisations. And carrying out of innovations is a function *sui generis* and this requires creative response to objective opportunities; this type of response is not dependent on previous increase in effective demand or markets. For Schumpeter, the market expands as a result of innovations introduced by entrepreneurs, who are capable of perceiving new opportunities that cannot be proved at the moment at which action has to be taken and who have supernormal energy and will power to break down the resistance that the social environment offers to change.

Such innovations, once introduced, compel other frills to adapt themselves to the new situation. Thus, adaptive response is

---

5. Ibid., p. 61.
6. Hicks, John (1969). *A Theory of Economic History*, Oxford: Oxford University Press.

subsequent to the spontaneous creative response of entrepreneurs. Market size expands because of the cumulative impact of these two types of responses to objective opportunities. This process is neither impersonal nor automatic and its outcome is *ex-ante* indeterminate. Hence, no rigorous analytical model of the process can be formulated.

Because of what he calls the "process of creative destruction", the nature and character of competition are quite different from what mainstream economists emphasised. To quote:[7]

> The first thing to go is the traditional conception of the *modus operandi* of (price) competition ... But in capitalist reality as distinguished from its textbook picture, it is not that kind of competition which counts but competition from the new commodity; the new technology, the new source of supply, the new type of organisation—competition which commands a decisive cost or quality advantage and which strikes not at the margins of the profits and outputs of existing firms but at their foundations and their very lives. This kind of competition is as much more effective than the other, as a bombardment is in comparison with forcing a door, and so much more important that it becomes a matter of comparative indifference whether competition in the ordinary sense functions more or less promptly; the powerful lever that in the long run expands output and brings down prices is in any case made of other stuff ... It is hardly necessary to point out that competition of the kind we now have in mind, acts not only when in being, but also when it is merely an ever-present threat.

Note that the idea of a contestable market is quite old and is not a new discovery.

In this process of creative destruction, monopolistic practices are "often unavoidable incidents, of a long-run process of expansion which they protect rather than impede. There is no more paradox in this than there is in saying that motor cars are travelling faster than they otherwise would, because they are provided with brakes."[8]

The entrepreneurial function, according to Schumpeter:

> ... need not be embodied ... in a particular individual. Every social environment has its own ways of filling this function. For instance, the practice of farmers in the USA has been revolutionised again and

7. Schumpeter, Joseph A. (1950). *Capitalism, Socialism and Democracy*. New York: Harper & Row. pp.84–85.
8. Ibid., p.88.

> again by the introduction of methods worked out in the Department of Agriculture, and by the Department's success in teaching these methods. In this case, then, it was the Department of Agriculture that acted as an entrepreneur. Again, the entrepreneurial function may be and often is filled cooperatively. With the development of large corporations, this has become of major importance: aptitudes that no single individual combines, can be built into a corporate personality.[9]

He also notes how this function was performed by the State in German principalities before German unification. To quote:

> The state—the Prince and his bureaucracy—not only meant more than, but also something different from, what they meant in other countries, and that one of the consequences of this was not only regulation of industry that amounted to guidance, but also actual state enterprise. The social structure that supplied the personnel of public administration was... much superior in intelligence, horizon, training and energy to the personnel of such private industry as then was; and this is one of the reasons why it would be as silly to condemn that public planning in the Germany of that time as it would be to hold it up as a model for societies of different structure. That the states built the canals and the roads which in England were created by private enterprise was natural under the circumstances... Much more interesting, however, is the entrepreneurial activity of principalities in the field of mining and its technological neighbours...Here initiative as well as execution came almost entirely from the princes and their bureaucracy...These entrepreneurs were public servants and acted by virtue of official appointment, but both in type and behaviour entirely conform to the idea of a 'captain of industry'. The central authority left them remarkably free to act, and in most cases ratified their plans as a matter of course.[10]

Much before Schumpeter, Marx's vision of the evolutionary process under capitalism was similar. He had a deep insight into the working of the capitalist process. For him as for Schumpeter, capitalism is a process characterised by constant revolutions of production; stationary capitalism—the idea of Ricardo-Mill-Marshall—would be a *contradictio in adjecto*. In the *Communist Manifesto* he writes: "constant revolutionising of production,

---

9. Schumpeter, A. Joseph, "Economic Theory and Entrepreneurial History", in *Essays*, n.2.

10. Schumpeter, A. Joseph (1939). *Business Cycles, Vol. 1*. New York: McGraw Hill. pp.283–84.

uninterrupted disturbance of all social conditions, everlasting uncertainty and agitation distinguish the bourgeois epoch from all other ones."[11] Innovations are then inherent in the process of economic evolution. They are the vehicle for the process of capital accumulation. He perceived the process of economic change more clearly than anybody else during his time. And he came very near to saying that this process of innovation was the result of the creative response of entrepreneurs to the environment. To quote Schumpeter:

> After having blocked out the historical background of capitalist development in a few strong strokes that are substantially correct, Marx launched a panegyric upon bourgeois achievement that has no equal in economic literature. The bourgeoisie 'has been the first to show what man's activity can bring about. It has accomplished wonders far surpassing Egyptian pyramids, Roman aqueducts, and Gothic cathedrals' and 'by the rapid improvement of all instruments of production...draws all nations, even the most barbarian into civilisation...it has created more massive and colossal productive forces than have all preceding generations together' and so forth. No reputable bourgeois economist of that or any other time—certainly not Adam Smith or J.S. Mill—ever said as much as this. Observe in particular, the emphasis on the creative role of the businessman, and of the business class as such, that the majority of 'bourgeois' economists so persistently overlooked. But even having got this far, most of us would, on the one hand, insert into the picture, nonbourgeois contributions to the success of the bourgeoisie—the contributions of nonbourgeois bureaucracy for instance; and, on the other hand, commit the mistake (for such I believe it is) to list science and technology as independent factors, where Marx's sociology enabled him to see that these factors, as well as progress in such fields as education and hygiene, were just as much products of the bourgeois class culture—and hence ultimately of the business class itself—as was business performance narrowly defined.[12]

Even Schumpeter, through a different analytic route, seems to agree substantially with Marx.

> Without going into this, we will notice that, primarily a product of the evolution of economic rationality, the cost-profit calculus in turn

---

11. *A Handbook of Marxism*. New York: Random House. 1935. p. 26.

12. Schumpeter, A. Joseph, "The Communist Manifesto in Sociology and Economics". in *Essays*. n.2, pp.292–93.

> reacts upon that rationality; by crystallising and defining numerically, it powerfully propels the logic of enterprise. And thus defined and quantified for the economic sector, this type of logic or attitude or method then starts upon its conqueror's career subjugating—rationalising—man's tools and philosophies, his medical practice, his picture of the cosmos, his outlook on life, everything in fact, including his concepts of beauty and justice and his spiritual ambitions ... In this respect it is highly significant that modern mathemetico-experimental science developed, in the fifteenth, sixteenth and seventeenth centuries, not only along with the social process usually referred to as the Rise of Capitalism, but also outside of the fortress of scholastic thought and in the face of its contemptuous hostility ... Not only the modern mechanised plant and the volume of the output that pours forth from it, not only modern technology and economic organisation, but all the features and achievements of modern civilisation are, directly or indirectly the products of the capitalist process.[13]

Note that for both Marx and Schumpeter, politics and policies as well as science and technology are not exogenous factors but are an integral part of the process of socio-economic evolution. Mainstream economists have still not recognised fully the endogenous character of these factors simply because they cannot be made part of a rigorous analytical model.

Thus, both recognise the achievements of the capitalist order and its historical necessity in the process of social evolution. However, neither likes the social values and the civilisation which the evolving capitalist process creates. For Marx, capitalism is a system of increasing exploitation and poverty of the working classes; this prognosis has not proved to be correct but that is the aspect of the system which he hates. Schumpeter's value judgement too is not favourable.

> As regards the economic performance, it does not follow that men are 'happier' or even 'better off' in the industrial society of today than they were in a medieval manor or village. As regards the cultural performance, one may accept every word I have written and yet hate it—its utilitarianism and the wholesale destruction of meanings incident to it—from the bottom of one's heart ... one may care less for the efficiency of the capitalist process in producing

13. Schumpeter. n.7. pp.124-125.

> economic and cultural values than for the kind of human beings that it turns out and then leaves to their own devices, free to make a mess of their lives.
>
> However, whether favorable or unfavorable, value judgements about capitalist performance are of little interest. For mankind is not free to choose ... Things economic and social move by their own momentum and the ensuing situations compel individuals and groups to behave in certain ways whatever they may wish to do—not indeed by destroying their freedom of choice but by shaping the choosing mentalities and by narrowing the list of possibilities from which to choose. If this is the quintessence of Marxism then all of us have got to be Marxists. In consequence, capitalist performance is not even relevant for prognosis.[14]

Thus, both Marx and Schumpeter are interested in the logic of the historical processes of socioeconomic change. Marx tried to formulate the logic of social evolution—what Schumpeter calls the grandiose logic of things historical—and the result was what is called "Economic Interpretation of History", which can be put into two propositions: (a) The technical conditions of production are the fundamental determinants of social structures—including politics and policies; and (b) the forms of production themselves have a logic of their own; that is to say, they change according to necessities inherent in them so as to produce their successors merely by their own working. Marx's economic interpretation of history does not mean that human beings are wholly or partially actuated by economic motives; what it means is that non-economic motives and institutions are shaped and conditioned by technical and social conditions governing productive activity. Men, of course, "choose" their course of action out of a variety of motives and their choice is not directly enforced by objective data of the environment; but they choose from standpoints, views and propensities that do not form another set of independent data but are themselves moulded by the objective set.[15]

Schumpeter regards this sociological proposition as "one of the greatest individual achievements of sociology to this day."[16] However,

---

14. Ibid. pp.129–130.
15. Ibid. p.12.
16. Ibid. p.10.

he notes social structures and related value systems, once formed, persist possibly for centuries and hence at any given point of time the dominant forms of the productive process cannot fully explain actual group attitudes and behaviour. For example, the social structure under the capitalist order right until 1914 in Europe represented not the structure one would expect on the basis of social and technological conditions; it represented a symbiosis of the feudal and capitalist structures. However, he thinks that the economic process has been the prime mover of social evolution in the industrial countries after the First World War. Thus, Marx's economic interpretation, according to him, appears to be currently valid.

Both regard capitalist institutional framework and motivation as a phase in social evolution and both show through their different analytical structures that the capitalist process, by the working of its inherent logic, would tend to destroy the foundations of the capitalist order and lead to the emergence of some sort of socialist order, after the creative role of the capitalist process is completed—that is in the fullness of time. The way in which Marx has analytically implemented his vision has turned out to be faulty. However, his vision may still be true:

> The idea of a theory, not merely of an indefinite number of disjointed individual patterns or of the logic of economic quantities in general, but of the actual sequence of those patterns or of the economic process, as it goes on, under its own steam, in historic time, producing at every instant that state which will of itself determine the next one ... He was the first economist of top rank to see and to teach systematically how economic theory may be turned into historical analysis and how the historical narrative be turned into *histoire raisonnée* ... Marx's economic theory succeeds in implementing his sociological set up. It does not succeed; but in failing, it establishes a goal and a method.[17]

This is the judgement of Schumpeter.

Economic Backwardness in Historical Perspective

Let me now turn to Gerschenkron's historical interpretation of European industrialisation during 1850 to 1914, that is after the industrial revolution in England had already made her the most

17. Ibid. pp.43–44.

industrially advanced country in Europe. His major thesis is that the pattern and process of industrialisation during that period in relatively backward countries like France, Germany and Russia were quite different from those of England. Thus, he rejects the concept of preconditions or set prerequisites for the industrialisation process. All these relationships mentioned as prerequisites

> Appear so logical, so compelling that one is indeed tempted to regard them in the light of historical necessity and to draw the conclusion that in cases where these prerequisites were lacking no industrialisation could take place. The only difficulty is that these beautiful exercises in logic have been defeated by history. They are not consistent with crude empiricism and are damaged seriously when confronted with the relevant facts as we know them.[18]

The relatively backward countries do evolve what he calls "substitutes for missing prerequisites" which are in the nature of creative innovations. The nature and character of such innovations depend critically on the degree of relative backwardness of a country. His "basic proposition is that within each of the individual countries in Europe certain specific features of the industrialisation process depended on the level of relative backwardness of the countries concerned on the eve of the period of great accelerations in their industrial growth."[19] These specific features relate to the speed and character of industrialisation processes, the specific institutional instruments and the intellectual climate; the intensity of these features depends on the degree of relative backwardness of the country.

The backward countries have one great asset and that is evolving modern technology.

> If as an empirical fact many smaller areas, such as some European countries, did show a strong leaning towards rapidly increasing output of heavy industries, there was a specific reason: it was within the field of these industries that the contemporaneous technological progress had been most vehement and backward countries often did tend to favor branches of industrial endeavors in which the most modern technology could be applied ... This tendency was frequently strongly reinforced by state and banking policies ... historical experience suggests a strong propensity on the part of backward

18. Gerschenkron, Alexander (1970). *Europe in the Russian Mirror*. Cambridge: Cambridge University Press. pp.100-101.
19. Ibid. pp.98-99.

> countries to apply the most modern technological processes, not yet introduced in more advanced countries. That there are both exceptions and limits to this is another matter.[20]
>
> Under the conditions the statement may be hazarded that, to the extent that industrialisation took place, it was largely by application of the most modern and efficient techniques that backward countries could hope to achieve success particularly if their industrialisation preceded in the face of the competition from the advanced country.[21]

This fact was largely responsible for their speed of growth as well as the stress on bigness of plant and enterprise.

Backward countries quite often lack adequate entrepreneurial talents as well as sources of financing large modern enterprises. These two obstacles or lack of prerequisites are generally overcome by what he calls institutional instruments or innovations. In countries where relative backwardness was moderate as in France and Germany, the institutional innovation was that of Credit Mobilier of the brothers Pereires or the Universal Bank:

> In particular, the story of the Credit Mobilier of the brothers Pereires is often regarded as a dramatic but, on the whole, rather insignificant episode ... It seems to be much better in accord with the facts to speak of a truly momentous role of investment banking of the period of the economic history of France and of large portions of the continent ... But more important than their slavish imitations was the creative adaptation of the basic idea of the Perieres and its incorporation in the new type of banks, the Universal Bank, which in Germany, along with most of the countries on the continent, became the dominant form of banking. The difference between banks of the Credit Mobilier type and commercial banks in the advanced industrial country of the time (England) was absolute. Between the English banks essentially designed to serve as a source of short-term capital and a bank designed to finance the long-term investment needs of the economy, there was a complete gulf. The German banks, which may be taken as a paragon of the type of Universal Bank, successfully continued the basic idea of the Credit Mobilier with the short-run activities of commercial banks.

---

20. Gerschenkron, Alexander (1968). *Continuity in History and Other Essays*. Cambridge, Mass.: Harvard University Press. pp.403-404.

21. Gerschenkron, Alexander (1962). *Economic Backwardness in Historical Perspective*. Cambridge, Mass.: Harvard University Press. p.89.

> But the German banks, and with them the Austrian and Italian banks, established the closest possible relations with industrial enterprises. A German bank, as the saying went, accompanied an industrial enterprise from the cradle to the grave, from establishment to liquidation through all the vicissitudes of its existence. Through the device of formally short-term but in reality long-term current account credits and through development of the institution of supervisory boards to the position of most powerful organs within corporate organisations, the banks acquired a formidable degree of ascendancy over industrial enterprises, which extended far beyond the sphere of financial control into that of entrepreneurial and management decisions. Continental practices in the field of industrial investment banking must be conceived as specific instruments of industrialiation in a backward country.[22]

The institutional instrument in a more backward country like Czarist Russia or Hungary was the role of the State. The industrialisation spurt in Russia (1880–1900) came almost thirty years after Germany and her backwardness was such that it was not possible to establish investment banks.

> The great industrial upswing came when, from the middle of eighties on, the railroad building of the state assumed unprecedented proportions and became the main lever of a rapid industrialisation policy. Through multifarious devices such as preferential orders to domestic producers of railroad materials, high prices, subsidies, credits, and profit guarantees to new industrial enterprises, the government succeeded in maintaining a high and, in fact, increasing rate of growth until the end of the century. Concomitantly, the Russian taxation system was reorganised, and the financing of industrialisation policies was thus provided for, while the stabilisation of the ruble and the introduction of the gold standard assured foreign participation in the development of Russian industry.[23]

It is worth emphasising that the nature of institutional instruments changes with what Gerschenkron calls "diminution of backwardness".

> At the turn of the century, if not somewhat earlier, changes became apparent in the relationship between German banks and German

22. Ibid. pp.11–16.
23. Ibid. p.19.

> industry. As the former industrial infants had grown to strong manhood, the original undisputed ascendancy of the banks over industrial enterprises could no longer be maintained ... The conditions of capital scarcity to which the German banks owed their historical position were no longer present. Germany had become a developed industrial country. But the specific features engendered by a process of industrialisation in condition of backwardness were to remain, and so was the close relation between banks and industry, even though the master-servant relation gave way to cooperation among equals and sometimes was even reversed.[24]

Similarly in Russia after 1905, when Russia again achieved a high rate of industrial growth between 1907–1914, the significance of the State was very greatly reduced and its place was taken by German-type universal banks. "In short, after the economic backwardness of Russia had been reduced by state-sponsored industrialisation process, use of a different instrument of industrialisation, suitable to the new 'state of backwardness' became applicable."[25]

What about the intellectual climate or industrialisation ideology, which motivated the process? Gerschenkron stresses the role of a socialist ideology of Saint-Simon in France.

> A large proportion of the men who reached positions of economic and financial influence upon Napoleon III's advent to power were not isolated individuals. They belonged to a rather well-defined group. They were not Bonapartists but Saint-Simonian socialists. The fact that a man like Isaac Pereiere, who contributed so much ... to the spread of the modern capitalist system in France should have been an ardent admirer of Saint-Simonian doctrines is on the face of it surprising ... It is more relevant to point the stress laid by Saint-Simon and his followers upon industrialisation and the great task they had assigned to banks as an instrument of organisation and development of the economy. This, no doubt, greatly appealed to the creators of the Credit Mobilier, who liked to think of their institution as a 'bank to a higher power' and of themselves as 'missionaries' rather than bankers ... Saint-Simonian ideas most decisively influenced the course of economic events inside and outside France. But the question remains: Why was the socialist garment draped around an essentially capitalist idea? And why was it the socialist

24. Ibid. p.21.
25. Ibid. p.22.

> form that was so readily accepted by the greatest capitalist entrepreneurs France ever possessed? ... It would seem that the answer must again be given in terms of basic conditions of backwardness .... under French conditions a *laissez-faire* ideology was altogether inadequate as a spiritual vehicle of an industrialisation program.[26]
>
> Similarly, Friedrich List's industrialisation theories may be largely conceived as an attempt, by a man whose personal ties to Saint-Simonians had been very strong, to translate the inspirational message of Saint-Simonism into a language that would be accepted in the German environment, where the lack of both a preceding political revolution and an early national unification rendered nationalist sentiment a much more suitable ideology of industrialisation.[27]
>
> After what has been just said it will perhaps not seem astonishing that in the Russian industrialisation of the 1890s, orthodox Marxism can be said to have performed a very similar function. Nothing reconciled the Russian intelligentsia more to the advent of capitalism in the country ... than a system of ideas which presented the capitalist industrialisation of the country as the result of an iron law of historical development ... In conditions of Russian 'absolute' backwardness, again, a much more powerful ideology was required to grease the intellectual and emotional wheels of industrialisation than either in France or Germany.[28]

It is pertinent to refer to his assessment of the period called Mercantilism. Hicks mentions in his *A Theory of Economic History* that "Mercantilism was a failure." This terse judgement, Gerschenkron argues, must not go unchallenged.

> In Hecksher's words mercantilism must be and seen as the period connecting the Middle Ages with the *laissez-faire* era, a statement that is correct not only chronologically but also substantively ... If a uniform concept, valid for the whole of the European continent, is desired, mercantilism must be defined as a policy of economic development, conducted by the state in the interest of the state. Mercantilist statesmen from Colbert to Peter the Great were first of all the great unifiers, the policies of unification being both physical

26. Ibid. pp.23–24.
27. Ibid. p.25.
28. Ibid.

> and institutional: creation of a vast network of roads and canals; unification (and stabilisation) of weights and measures; and the first serious attempts to abolish barriers to trade in the form of tariffs and tolls within the territory of the individual states, thus creating large market and 'mercantilising' the economy ... In addition, one must mention the progress achieved in increasing the resources of the economy and in their transformation by the industrial policies of the mercantilist regimes and their attempts to diversify the goods produced and to increase their quality, thus greatly deepening the nature of the markets. Economic development conducted under the aegis of the 'immortal' state naturally contributed to a considerable risk in time horizons, even though the clash between investment and immediate military expenditure was being fought out throughout the mercantilist period. In short, it was at least just as much the policies of the state as the activities of the merchants that laid the ground both for subsequent great spurts of industrial development (metaphorically described as revolutions) and for the advent of *laissez- faire* policies.[29]

Gerschenkron mentions the opportunity of absorbing modern technology as the great "advantage" the backward countries have. However, it is not inevitable that this objective opportunity is always seized. In this connection, he has a concept of a "nodal point", beyond which the advantages of backwardness are offset by the growing disadvantages of backwardness—greater stress on equality and egalitarian policies in general and the resulting social tensions and strife, even before the industrialisation process gathers momentum. This happened in Italy (1881–1913), when the State could not play its "expected" role and further pursued protectionist policies, dictated by the vested interests, which slowed down the speed of growth by discriminating against those industries which had the best prospects for growth.

In Bulgaria (1878–1937), too, the State did not play its "expected" role, because the government of the time preferred to allocate most of its budgetary means to its military expenditures, in order to satisfy its territorial aspirations towards the shores of the Aegean and in Macedonia, getting finally involved in the disastrous adventure of the Second Balkan War. The opportunity, thus, was missed.

---

29. Gerschenkron, Alexander (1971). "Mercator Glorious", *Economic History Review*. November.

It is worth noting his research with regard to the emergence of entrepreneurs. There is a popular school of thought emanating from Max Weber's theses (witness the debate about achieving and not-achieving societies) which relates the emergence of entrepreneurs to a certain value system. Gerschenkron corroborates Schumpeter's finding that private entrepreneurs are likely to emerge from all layers and classes of society, irrespective of value systems. Entrepreneurs did emerge even in a social-cultural climate inimical to them in Russia during 1880–1914. Historically, the experience has been that unless a certain traditional pre-industrial value system gets formalised and crystallised in the shape of government policy, it has little influence on the emergence of the entrepreneurial class.

Gerschenkron notes that the story of European industrialisations in the nineteenth century would seem to yield a few points of view which may be helpful for appreciation of current problems in developing countries: One of his striking and illuminating observations is the following:

> What makes it so difficult for an advanced country to appraise properly the industrialisation policies of its less fortunate brethren is the fact that, in every instance of industrialisation, imitation of the evolution in advanced countries appears in combination with different, indigenously determined elements. If it is not always easy for advanced countries to accept the former, it is even more difficult for them to acquiesce in the latter. This is particularly true of the institutional instruments used in carrying out industrial developments and even more so of ideologies which accompany it. What can be derived from a historical review is a strong sense for the significance of the native elements in the industrialisation of backward countries ... A journey through the last century may, by destroying what Bertrand Russell once called the 'dogmatism of the untraveled', help in formulating a broader and more enlightened view of the pertinent problems and in replacing the absolute notions of what is 'right' and what is 'wrong' by a more flexible and relativistic approach.[30]

I may mention that the validity of his approach of relating the specific features of the industrialisation pattern and process to the degree of relative backwardness of a country is borne out by the experience of Japan during 1870–1900 as well as after the Second

30. Gerschenkron n.21, pp.26–27.

World War and the experience of the East Asian countries after 1960. I refer in this connection to the well-documented study of Rosovsky on Japan (1868–1940), in which the validity of Gerschenkron's approach is explicitly discussed, the World Bank's *East Asian Miracle* and recent studies on *The Japanese Main Bank System, The Japanese Civil Service and Economic Development* and *The Role of Government in East Asian Development.*[31]

Concluding Observations

Thus ends the story of what I consider to be the most profound insights or visions with regard to the development process. I have narrated the story rather briefly, though I have deliberately used the authors' own words to draw pointed attention to certain significant ideas. These insights raise questions about potential factors and potential relationships among them and thus help us in understanding and appreciating the development process in backward countries, including our own. However, they do not—cannot—provide any answers.

For as they show, the relationship between economic and non-economic factors changes over time in a given country and is different in different countries. Hence, it is not possible to formulate in general terms uniform policies and strategies, applicable to all the countries in terms of any economic or social theory—be it neoclassical or what is now pompously called new growth economics—or the development experience of one country or another. One cannot be dogmatic about the role of the State also for it depends on a specific historical context and a specific social situation. The policies which succeed at one time create, through the inherent logic of the social process of development, different types of challenges, to which creative adaptation does not always materialise. Thus, the evolutionary processes are neither smooth nor continuous; the outcome is always *ex-ante* indeterminate. Hence, it is not possible to formulate in quantitative terms any rigorous model of the process. Any strategy or policy has unintended consequences.

31. Rosovsky, Henry (1961). *Capital Formation in Japan, 1868-1940*, Glencoe; World Bank (1993). *The East Asian Miracle: Economic Growth and Public Policy*. Oxford: Oxford University Press; Aoki, M. and Hugh Patrick (eds.) (1994). *The Japanese Main Bank System: Its Relevance for Developing and Transforming Economies*. Oxford: Oxford University Press; Hyung-Ki Kim *et al.* (eds.) (1995). *The Japanese Civil Service and Economic Development*. Oxford: Clarendon Press; M. Aoki *et al.* (eds.) (1997). *The Role of Government in East Asian Economic Development*. Oxford: Clarendon Press.

One generalisation which one can make is that the nature and character of the process inevitably depends on the nature and quality of leadership in the political, economic and cultural spheres and their ability for creative response to the emerging challenges of development. This, of course, is obvious but nonetheless true. How and when such leadership emerges in time is a mystery; the past bequeaths the present while the aspect of the future remains uncertain.

Index

I

J

K

L

U

V

W

Y

ABOUT THE AUTHOR

V.V. Bhatt

Dr. V.V. Bhatt, educated at the University of Bombay and Harvard University where he was a teaching fellow while working on his Ph.D. dissertation in 1951-52, had a successful career both as an academic and a national and international civil servant. As an inspiring teacher of economics, he distinguished himself at one of the constituent colleges of the University of Bombay, the United Nations Institute for Social and Economic Development, Bangkok and, the World Bank Economic Institute, Washington D.C.

As a frequently cited economic researcher, he published some of his seminal articles on capital-output ratios, choice of techniques, balanced and unbalanced growth, project evaluation, income-distribution in India—all major topics in the evolving discipline of development economics. He chose for exegesis of his ideas internationally acclaimed peer-reviewed journals such as *The American Economic Review, The Review of Economics and Statistics, Economic Journal, The Oxford Bulletin of Economics and Statistics, Economic Development and Cultural Change, Kyklos, The Journal of Development Studies, Economia Internazionale, World Development, Economic and Political Weekly* etc.

He authored nine books on economics among which *Employment and Capital Formation in Underdeveloped Economies* (Bombay: Orient Longman. 1960), *A Framework for Planned Economic Development of Lower Mekong Countries* (Bangkok: United Nations. 1966), *Development Perspectives* (Oxford: Pergamon Press. 1980) and *Financial Systems, Innovations and Development* (New Delhi and London: Sage Publications and Thousand Oaks. 1995) figure prominently.

As a public servant, he held high positions such as Economic Adviser, Reserve Bank of India and Chief Executive in the Industrial Bank of India and also Chief, Public Finance Division in the World Bank.